FOURTH EDITION

The Collectors Encyclopedia of

DEPRESSION GLASS

BY

Gene Florence

COLLECTOR BOOKS

Published by Collector Books
Box 3009
Paducah, Kentucky, 42001

ABOUT THE AUTHOR

Gene FLorence, Jr., was born in Lexington, Kentucky, in 1944 and received his A.B. from the University of Kentucky in 1967, having majored in Mathematics and English. After teaching nine years in the Kentucky school systems, he left that to pursue his interest in glass to a greater extent.

He helped his mother convert her children's day nursery into Grannie Bear Antique Shop, the name being a holdover of the endearing term the 30 or so toddlers gave her. Naturally, should you be in Lexington, he'd appreciate your visiting that shop located at 120 Clay Avenue. As he's often there, you might meet him.

Mr. Florence has been interested in "collecting" since childhood, beginning with the usual baseball cards and comic books and advancing to coin collecting, bottles and, finally, glassware.

He has written other books on glassware, the Collector's Encyclopedia of Akro Agate, the Collector's Encyclopedia of Occupied Japan, and the Pocket Guide to Depression Glass, which have received warm praises from collectors in these fields.

Should you know of any unlisted pieces of glassware **in the patterns shown in this book** please feel free to write him: Gene Florence, P.O. Box 7186H, Lexington, Kentucky 40522. Please enclose a self addressed stamped envelope if you wish a reply.

ACKNOWLEDGEMENTS

I could write a separate book on the things that went wrong while trying to get this book together. However, the following people are a part of the everything right portion of the book. They lent their time, their skill, their homes, their glass; and I am most humbly grateful to each and every one:

Thank you: Cathy: wife, typist, editor, sounding board; Sons: Chad and Marc, for almost managing the quiet necessary; Family: Dad, Mom, Charles, Sib, Marie, Tim, for caring for children, home and animals on our frequent trips, and Lois, for spending vacation time proof reading; Friends: John and Trannie Davis, Earl and Beverly Hines, Kelly and Priscilla McBride, who lent glass and opened their home to the furor of a photography session; Helen Marshall, Irene Gilcrest, Arlene Showalter, Iris Slayton and Sam Collings, who lent glass, time and knowledge;Members of the Peach State Depression Club: Joe Loudermilk for photography, Mary Ensley, Claude and Betty Pickelsimer, Joe and Jane Damiano, Jerry and Donna Stoner, Albert and Edna Freeman, Ed Chagnon, Jenny Fender, Ray and Vicki Hejl, Millie Smith, Joan Evans, Ray and Lawana Smith, Enzull Cole, Barbara Moore, Peggy Crawford, Karen Asherbranner for gathering up, lending and even delivering glass to be photographed; Photographer, James Burke of Burke Studio in Lexington who took the new pictures for the book.

There is always the possibility of leaving someone out in a listing of that sort. If I have, it wasn't intentional nor am I unappreciative of your help. It's just as we go to press on this edition, I've overlooked your gesture of kindness. Forgive me if I have and be happy in the fact that many people are enjoying your contribution to this book.

Index

FOREWORD

Depression Glass as defined in this book is the colored glassware made primarily during the Depression years in the colors of amber, green, pink, blue, red, yellow, white and crystal. There are other colors and some glass included which was made before, as well as after this time; but primarily, the glass within this book was made from late 1920's through the 1930's. More attention is being given to some of the hand made glass of late, but mostly this book is concerned with the inexpensively made glassware turned out in quantity and given away as promotions or inducements to buy other products during that era known as The Depression.

Since the issuance of the past three editions which have gone past the 100,000 mark in circulation, there have been changes in the collecting of Depression Glass. More and more attention is now being given the cheaper priced patterns and collectors are becoming aware of the better glassware made during this same period of time. There are several such patterns included in this book.

Information gathered for the book has come from research, experience, fellow dealers, and over 200,000 miles of travel in connection with glassware as well as from readers who were kind enough and interested enough to share their knowledge with me. This last I particularly appreciate.

Descriptions of the cover pieces are on the last page of this book.

PRICING

ALL PRICES IN THIS BOOK ARE RETAIL PRICES FOR MINT CONDITION GLASSWARE. THIS BOOK IS INTENDED TO BE ONLY A GUIDE TO PRICES AS THERE ARE SOME REGIONAL PRICE DIFFERENCES WHICH CANNOT REASONABLY BE DEALT WITH HEREIN.

You may expect dealers to pay from thirty to fifty percent less than the prices quoted. Glass that is in less than mint condition, i.e. chipped, cracked, scratched or poorly molded, will bring very small prices unless extremely rare; and then, will bring only a small percentage of the price of glass that is in mint condition.

Prices have become pretty well nationally standardized due to national advertising carried on by dealers and due to the Depression Glass Shows which are held from coast to coast. However, **there are still some regional differences in prices due** partly **to glass being more readily available in some areas than in others.** Too, companies distributed certain pieces in some areas that it did not in others. Generally speaking, however, prices are about the same among dealers from coast to coast.

Prices tend to increase dramatically on rarer items and, in general, they have increased as a whole due to more and more collectors entering the field and people becoming more aware of the worth of Depression Glass.

One of the more important aspects of this book is the attempt made to illustrate as well as realistically price those items which are in demand. The desire was to give you the most accurate guide to collectible patterns of Depression Glass available.

MEASUREMENTS

To illustrate why there are discrepancies in measurements, I offer the following sample from just two years of Hocking's catalogue references:

Year	Pitcher Ounces	Flat Tumbler Ounces	Footed Tumbler Ounces
1935	37, 58, 80	5, 9, 13½	10, 13
1935	37, 60, 80	5, 9, 10, 15	10, 13
1936	37, 65, 90	5, 9, 13½	10, 15
1935	37, 60, 90	5, 9, 13½	10, 15

All measurements in this book are exact as to some manufacturer's listing or to actual measurement. You may expect variance of up to ½ inch or 1-5 ounces. This may be due to mold variation or changes made by the manufacturer.

ADAM JEANNETTE GLASS COMPANY, 1932-1934

Colors: Pink, green, crystal, yellow

No different pieces of Adam pattern have surfaced since the writing of the third book. This pattern, however, still has the distinction of containing some of the rarest of the rare because of the **round** shaped pieces which have been found in both pink and yellow. (Novices will please note that the pattern generally has a squared shape; hence the fervor over finding pieces with the Adam motif clearly stated on rounded plates and saucers). These round pieces were undoubtedly experimental pieces made at the factory since so few have surfaced. To date, rounded **yellow** pieces outnumber rounded **pink** ones; all pieces number fewer than two dozen. Thus, it's safe to say that if you own one of these, you have an extremely rare piece of Depression Glass. These items are pictured.

Major price advances have occurred in the pink vase and the 5½" iced tea tumblers. If you have not grabbed dinner plates, cereal bowls and even cups and saucers which you need for your set, I would strongly advise you to do so at once else you'll be certain to feel you're buying fine china at the prices being asked. Perhaps those plain tumblers having the panels and curves of regular Adam, but not the motif, (originally found packaged with the round based pitcher in Adam) will turn out to have value after all. Heretofore, they have been shunned as "poor relation".

I still get letters on the Adam-Sierra butter dish so I'll repeat that in the Adam-Sierra combination butter dish, the Adam pattern is found on the **outside** of the butter top, the Sierra pattern is found imprinted on the **inside** of the butter top only. The size and shape of the tops for both patterns are identical.

The Adam lamp, which is shaped like the Floral lamp made by the same company, is still elusive. The lamp base was made from a frosted sherbet which was notched to accommodate a switch. The bulb and cover, of course, are the most difficult parts to find — even should you get lucky and stumble across the base itself!

Lids to the sugar bowl and the candy dish in Adam are interchangeable.

I seldom say anything about crystal Adam other than the prices remain lower because of little demand. However, after seeing some published reports recently advocating that new collectors should start collections of this because it is still cheap, I feel compelled to point out that there are very few pieces of crystal Adam to be had. In the eight years I've been associated with this business, I've only seen five different pieces which the company even made; and probably I could count on my fingers and toes the total number of pieces of crystal Adam which I have even run across in all my travels. I think it's grossly unfair to suggest to newcomers to the field that they try to collect this pattern in crystal.

	Pink	Green		Pink	Green
Ash Tray, 4½"	8.50	9.00	Pitcher, 8", 32 oz.	17.50	20.00
Bowl, 4¾" Dessert	6.00	6.50	Pitcher, 32 oz., Round Base	22.50	
Bowl, 5¾" Cereal	9.50	10.50	Plate, 6" Sherbet	3.00	3.25
Bowl, 7¾"	8.00	8.50	**Plate, 7¾" Sq. Salad	5.00	6.25
Bowl, 9" Covered	20.00	42.50	Plate, 9" Sq. Dinner	9.50	10.50
Bowl, 10" Oval	11.00	12.50	Plate, 9" Grill	7.50	8.50
Butter Dish & Cover	57.50	187.50	Platter, 11¾"	8.00	8.50
Butter Dish Combination			Relish Dish, 8" Divided	5.50	6.50
with Sierra Pattern	437.50		Salt & Pepper, 4" Footed	31.50	62.50
Cake Plate, 10" Footed	8.00	8.50	***Saucer, Sq. 6"	2.75	3.00
Candlesticks, 4" Pair	32.50	47.50	Sherbet, 3"	8.75	9.50
Candy Jar & Cover 2½"	32.50	49.50	Sugar	8.00	8.50
Coaster 3¼"	8.50	8.75	Sugar/Candy Cover	8.50	12.50
Creamer	8.00	8.50	Tumbler, 4½"	9.50	10.50
*Cup	8.50	7.50	Tumbler, 5½" Iced Tea	21.50	20.00
Lamp	67.50	67.50	Vase, 7½"	57.50	25.00

```
  *Yellow        80.00
 **Round Pink   75.00    Yellow    80.00
***Round Pink   65.00    Yellow    70.00
```

Please refer to Foreword for pricing information

AKRO AGATE CO.
1913-1951

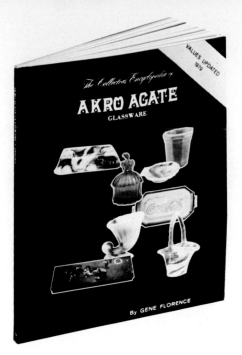

The story of Akro Agate was too big for the one page in the second edition to really do more than scratch the surface. Children's dishes constitute only a very small portion of the total picture. Thus it was, after some further research, I decided to write a book on that topic alone, something that wasn't too hard since there is such a wealth of material to be covered. Devotees of this glassware have been warm in their praises for my efforts I'm happy to report.

Akro Agate has a fascinating history which has its start before the first World War and continues throughout the war years. This all encompassing glassware is fast becoming a worthy collectible, a fact which is being mirrored in the prices, naturally. As with Collectors Encyclopedia of Depression Glass, should the book just save you from selling a piece too cheaply that you presently own or if it clues you to the real value of a piece you find at a sale, the knowledge gained will have certainly "paid for" the book.

If you are interested in collecting glassware, I feel sure you will enjoy and gain from this book on Akro Agate. Write me about your "finds" as I am equally interested in the oddities being discovered in this.

Copies of Akro Agate may be ordered from
COLLECTOR BOOKS
Box 3009, Paducah, Kentucky 42001
or
The Author, Gene Florence
P.O. Box 7186H
Lexington, Kentucky 40522
at $8.95 plus .60 postage for the first book
& .25 each additional copy
Dealers and Clubs write for quantity discounts

AMERICAN PIONEER LIBERTY WORKS 1931-1934

Colors: Pink, green, amber, crystal.

When I introduced this pattern into my third edition, I thought it would prove fairly easy to find once people saw the picture and started looking for it. However, this has not been the case. In fact, scarcity of pieces in all colors is proving to be a problem. I should qualify that by saying that the basic luncheon or bridge set items, i.e. cups, saucers, creamer, sugar, handled plate and large handled bowls, are readily available in many areas of the country. However, other items are proving very hard to get.

Crystal has gained little respectibility with collectors; again, only the luncheon ware is found in quantity.

The amber ball shaped lamp shown seems to be the only amber piece that is showing up.

New pieces discovered since the last listing are a 2¼", 2 oz. whiskey tumbler (shown with urn in pattern shot), a short sherbet matching the tall one pictured; and a 3½", 5 oz. juice tumbler.

Lids to candy dishes are interchangeable; the shorter, 1½ lb. candy is turning out to be the more difficult to get, however. The taller, 1 lb. candy is often confused with a vase, particularly if the candy is missing its lid (as mine now is thanks to some "help" I got setting up for a show! Oh, the help was fine; it was just that silly lid thinking it could fly that was the problem). The candy bottom is almost straight up at the top rim.

There are four styles of vases: straight edge (slightly curved out); rolled edge (sharply rolled out); curved in (rolled inward); scalloped edge. All four styles, so far, occur in pink.

The 4½" vase which holds 16 oz. and which I believe to be a rose bowl has been termed a mayonnaise also, though it seems large for a mayonnaise to me.

There are two sizes of covered casserole dishes, an 8¾" and a 9¼".

	Crystal, Pink	Green		Crystal, Pink	Green
Bowl, 5" handled	7.00	7.75	*Lamp, 5½" round, ball shape	45.00	
Bowl, 8¾" covered	47.50	57.50	Lamp, 8½" tall	47.50	62.50
Bowl, 9" handled	9.00	12.00	Pitcher, 5" covered urn	77.50	97.50
Bowl, console 10 3/8"	32.50	42.50	Pitcher, 7" covered urn	87.50	117.50
Candlesticks, 6½" pair	35.00	42.50	Plate, 8"	3.00	4.00
Candy Jar and Cover, 1 lb.	42.00	50.00	Plate, 11½" handled	6.00	7.50
Candy Jar and Cover, 1½ lb.	52.50	62.50	Saucer	2.00	3.50
Cheese and Cracker Set			Sherbet, 3½"	5.00	7.50
(indented platter and comport)	15.00	17.50	Sherbet, 4¾"	8.50	11.50
Coaster, 3½"	6.00	9.50	Sugar, 2¾"	3.00	5.00
Creamer, 2¾"	3.00	5.00	Sugar, 3½"	4.50	6.50
Creamer, 3½"	4.50	6.50	Tumbler, 5 oz. Juice	8.50	12.00
Cup	2.50	4.50	Tumbler, 4", 8 oz.	10.00	15.00
Dresser Set (2 cologne,			Tumbler, 5", 12 oz.	12.50	22.50
powder jar, on indented			Vase, rose bowl, 16 oz. 4¼",		
7½" tray)	47.50		ftd.	35.00	52.50
Goblet, Wine, 4", 3 oz.	11.50	15.00	Vase, 7", four styles,	47.50	67.50
Goblet, Water, 6", 8 oz.	12.50	17.50	Whiskey, 2¼" 2 oz.	27.50	32.50
Ice Bucket, 6"	16.50	19.50			

*Amber $57.50

Please refer to Foreword for pricing information

AMERICAN SWEETHEART MACBETH EVANS GLASS COMPANY 1930-1936

Colors: Pink, monax, red, blue; some cremax and color rimmed monax.

If something is monaxial in botany, it refers to plants flowering from a single axis. Looking at the center motif of this pattern, you can see the significance of that. How "monax" came to refer to just the milky white color of Depression Glass I don't know.

Those monax shakers you see hiding behind the pink bowl are few and far between; many collectors of the monax color are still seeking them for their set; hence, the price. The last pair of shakers I owned in this pattern came from a lady who purchased them at an auction. Nothing unusual in that--- except she bought 15 pair for $7.50 and among them were the monax American Sweetheart!

Monax sugar lids are another desirable item to own. At first, these were believed to be fewer than a dozen. However, more and more have been located; yet not enough to call them plentiful by any means!

Keep your eye peeled for two special monax bowls, a hat shaped one and a smaller version of the 18" console bowl.

Monax pieces are sometimes trimmed with red or gold bands.

Pink is the color most widely collected in this pattern. Difficult pieces to locate in pink include the 7½", 60 oz. (to brim) pitcher and the salt and pepper shakers which are more rarely found than the monax.

Notice the strange, tumbler-like vase pictured which has been found in pink. It's 4½" tall and is unique at this writing.

I have enlarged this pattern to four pages this year since the previous written material had to be set in such minuscule type as to make it difficult to read. **Please turn the page for further information on American Sweetheart.**

	Pink	Monax		Pink	Monax
Bowl, 3¾", Flat, Berry	12.50		Plate, 15½" Server		145.00
Bowl, 4½", Cream Soup	14.50	32.50	Platter, 13" Oval	13.50	29.50
Bowl, 6" Cereal	5.50	8.50	Pitcher, 7½", 60 oz.	247.50	
Bowl, 9" Round, Berry	10.50	27.50	Pitcher, 8", 80 oz.	197.50	
Bowl, 9½" Flat Soup	15.00	30.00	Salt and Pepper, Footed	175.00	177.50
Bowl, 11" Oval Vegetable	12.50	30.00	Saucer	2.00	2.25
Bowl, 18" Console		245.00	Sherbet, Footed, 4"	9.50	
Creamer, Footed	5.50	6.50	Sherbet, Footed, 4¼"		
Cup	5.50	7.00	(Design inside or outside)	6.50	10.00
Lampshade		300.00	Sherbet in Metal Holder (Crystal		
Plate, 6" Bread and Butter	1.50	3.25	Only) 3.00		
Plate, 8" Salad	4.50	5.50	Sugar, Open, Footed	4.50	5.50
Plate, 9" Luncheon		6.00	Sugar Cover (Monax Only)*		120.00
Plate, 9¾" Dinner	9.50	11.50	Tidbit 3 Tier, 8", 12" & 15½"		85.00
Plate, 10¼" Dinner	10.00	12.50	Tumbler, 3½", 5 oz.	20.00	
Plate, 11" Chop Plate		9.50	Tumbler, 4", 9 oz.	17.50	
Plate, 12" Salver	7.50	10.00	Tumbler, 4½", 10 oz.	19.50	

*Two style knobs.

Please refer to Foreword for pricing information

AMERICAN SWEETHEART (Con't.)

How do you like these unusual pink and green edged pieces of American Sweetheart which surfaced recently?

That overturned bowl and plate having the blue edging represent what is known as "Smoke" American Sweetheart. It seems extremely scarce and is perhaps the most desirable color to be found in this pattern.

Solid blue American Sweetheart is turning out to be a rarer color than the red. Blue and red sherbets with the American Sweetheart SHAPE have turned up. Since they haven't the design on them, they tend to be more interesting than rare.

Some American Sweetheart shakers have surfaced with fired-on colors of red, green and pink. Unfortunately, not being "true" color they have little appeal for collectors.

New items to appear in this pattern include a floor lamp with a cremax shade. What's so unusual? The brass base had matching panel grooves. In other words, you could line up the vertical lines on the shade with matching lines on the base! Cremax is a beige, clam-like color. A small bowl in cremax is pictured on the preceding page. Cups and saucers have also been found in this not so popular color.

In Canada an amber color lamp shade with the American Sweetheart design was found on a lamp having a brown pottery base!

Shades are sometimes found with orange, green, brown and blue panels of color fired-on over the design.

	Red	Blue	Cremax	Smoke & Other Trims
Bowl, 6" Cereal			7.00	17.50
Bowl, 9" Round, Berry			27.50	55.00
Bowl, 18" Console	475.00	550.00		
Creamer, Footed	75.00	85.00		37.50
Cup	75.00	85.00		35.00
Lampshade			350.00	
Lamp (Floor with Brass Base)			500.00	
Plate, 6" Bread and Butter				12.50
Plate, 8" Salad	62.50	80.00		20.00
Plate, 9" Luncheon				25.00
Plate, 9¾" Dinner				37.50
Plate, 10¼" Dinner				37.50
Plate, 12" Salver	125.00	150.00		
Plate, 15½" Server	230.00	275.00		
Platter, 13" Oval				65.00
Saucer	30.00	35.00		12.50
Sherbet, Footed, 4¼" (Design inside or outside)				22.50
Sugar, Open, Footed	75.00	85.00		37.50
Tidbit 3 Tier, 8", 12" & 15½"	325.00	425.00		

15

ANNIVERSARY JEANNETTE GLASS COMPANY 1947-1949

Colors: Pink (recently in crystal and iridescent)

Popularity of pink Anniversary is steadily increasing; however, demand for crystal remains nil except for the butter dish and cover.

The wine glass, 9" fruit bowl and the 12½" sandwich server are very hard to find.

I would remind readers that an iridescent issue of Anniversary is from the early 1970's and should be very moderately priced. Don't be duped by the ever present tale of the piece being "old" or so-called "Carnival" glass and therefore worth the way overboard price that's on it.

The listing below is from a Jeannette catalog of 1947. What we call today a "compote" they refer to as a "comport".

Anniversary is not, strictly speaking, glass from the Depression era; but, like some patterns made even into the early 1950's, it has become collectible.

	Crystal	Pink		Crystal	Pink
Bowl, 4 7/8" Berry	1.50	1.75	Plate, 6¼" Sherbet	1.25	1.50
Bowl, 7 3/8" Soup	3.00	4.00	Plate, 9" Dinner	2.50	3.75
Bowl, 9" Fruit	5.00	8.50	Plate, 12½" Sandwich Server	4.00	6.00
Butter Dish and Cover	25.00	32.50	Relish Dish, 8"	4.25	6.00
Candy Jar and Cover	10.00	20.00	Saucer	1.00	1.50
*Comport, Open, 3 Legged	2.25	3.50	Sherbet, Footed	2.50	4.00
Cake Plate, 12½"	5.50	8.00	Sugar	2.00	3.50
Cake Plate and Cover	10.00	12.50	Sugar Covers	2.50	4.00
Candlestick, 4 7/8" pair	10.00		Vase, 6½"	6.00	9.00
Creamer, Footed	2.75	4.00	Vase, Wall Pin-up	10.00	12.00
Cup	2.00	3.00	Wine Glass, 2½ oz.	5.50	8.50
Pickle Dish, 9"	3.75	4.50			

AUNT POLLY U.S. GLASS COMPANY

Colors: Blue, green, iridescent.

One discovery I wrote about in the trade publications since my last book was that the manufacturer of Aunt Polly and her sister patterns, Floral & Diamond and Strawberry, was probably U.S Glass Company rather than Jenkins Glass Company. This conclusion was reached after some careful sleuthing was done by Doug Lucas of the Three Rivers Depression Glass Club in Pittsburgh. I very much appreciate his sharing this information.

An Aunt Polly impersonator has been found in the form of a strange tumbler in green and blue. It is somewhat off regular color and slightly thinner in appearance than the regular Aunt Polly tumbler. Its green color is a kind of vaseline green as opposed to the normal shade (see Strawberry pattern for the correct shade of green) and its blue is lighter and more vivid than the Aunt Polly blue color shown.

The butter dish, pitcher, shakers, creamer and covered sugar are still avidly sought by collectors who do not collect whole sets of a pattern, but who collect just these pieces.

The oval bowl and shakers constitute quite a "find" in this particular pattern. You've heard of the expression "scarce as hen's teeth"?

	Green Iridescent	Blue		Green Iridescent	Blue
Bowl, 4 3/8" Berry	3.50	4.00	Creamer	12.50	15.00
Bowl, 4¾" 2" High	8.50	10.00	Pitcher, 8", 48 oz.		85.00
Bowl, 7¼" Oval, Handled			Plate, 6" Sherbet	2.00	2.75
Pickle	7.50	10.00	Plate, 8" Luncheon		5.00
Bowl, 7 7/8" Large Berry	8.50	10.00	Salt and Pepper		117.50
Bowl, 8 3/8" Oval	12.50	19.50	Sherbet	5.00	6.00
Butter Dish and Cover	137.50	92.50	Sugar	10.00	12.50
Candy, Cover, Two Handled	12.50	17.50	Sugar Cover	25.00	30.00
			Tumbler, 3 5/8", 8 oz.		10.00
			Vase, 6½", Footed	19.50	17.50

*Old form; presently called compote.
  Open compote or candy.

Please refer to Foreword for pricing information

17

AVOCADO, No. 601 INDIANA GLASS COMPANY 1923-1933

Colors: Pink, green, crystal.   *(See Reproduction Section)*

In 1973 Tiara Exclusive Home Products issued a pink pitcher and tumblers similar to the older pink Avocado and thereby stunted the growth of collecting the older pink Avocado for some time---even though the newer line of pink was a decidedly more orange color than the older glassware had been. In some sense, collecting pink Avocado has never been the same since even though the company only issued pitcher and tumbler sets.

This past year, the collecting of green Avocado has reached almost fad proportions; therefore, the announcement that Tiara was about to make green and frosted green pitcher and tumbler sets in 1979 was greeted by shudders from collectors and dealers alike as many feared this would do to green what had been done to pink in the past.

However, at this writing, I am happy to report that my source says the pitcher and tumblers in green are much darker green than were the old ones and that no one should have any difficulty in telling the two apart.

Do keep in mind that Tiara has only issued pitcher and tumbler sets. No other pieces are affected. **You may also wish to turn to the end of this book for an update on the colors put out in Avocado thus far by Tiara.**

You will notice there is a tremendous price jump in green Avocado from those listed in the past book; whether the issue of the green by Tiara will have any affect on these prices as time passes I have no way of foreseeing. It may be that the prices will be content to slow their pace to a walk rather than the jogging along they've been doing over the past year.

Be aware that there are three cups to be found for every saucer.

Older pitcher and tumblers in green are elusive.

The "apple" design plates, one pictured here, one in back of book in amber, are oddities that rarely show themselves.

Salad bowls and pitchers have been turning up in a milk glass white. I date these items from the middle 1950's when Indiana made some Sandwich glass in the white milk color.

Since the price of this pattern is presently on an upward spiral, I wouldn't be surprised at finding a few more pieces surfacing than have been previously known. Price sometimes has a way of turning up unknown pieces.

	Pink	Green		Pink	Green
Bowl, 5¼", Two-Handled	12.50	15.00	*Pitcher, 64 ozs.	250.00	400.00
Bowl, 6" Relish, Footed	13.00	16.50	Plate, 6¼" Sherbet	5.00	8.50
Bowl, 7" Preserve One Handle	11.00	13.50	**Plate, 8¼" Luncheon	9.00	12.50
Bowl, 7½" Salad	15.00	22.50	Plate, 10¼" Two Handled		
Bowl, 8" Oval, Two-Handled	13.00	17.00	Cake	19.50	27.50
Bowl, 8½" Berry	20.00	29.50	Saucer	15.50	20.00
Bowl, 9½", 3¼" Deep	35.00	47.50	Sherbet	32.50	47.50
Creamer, Footed	15.50	22.50	Sugar, Footed	15.50	22.50
Cup, Footed	20.00	23.50	*Tumbler	27.50	52.50

*Caution on pink. The orangeish-pink is new!
**Apple Design $10.00.   Amber $27.50.

Please refer to Foreword for pricing information

BEADED BLOCK   IMPERIAL GLASS COMPANY 1927-1930's

Colors: Pink, green, crystal, ice blue, vaseline, iridescent, amber, red and opalescent.

Imperial Glass Company still has the molds for this particular pattern. Iridized pink pieces and a white lily bowl turn up regularly. However, these are marked with the "IG" symbol in the bottom, a symbol Imperial has used only in about the last twenty years.

The pitcher which holds one pint has not been seen in amber.

Beaded Block is another pattern which does not have cups and saucers; going one better, it has no glasses either. Therefore, you find collectors of Beaded Block are "item" collectors; they search only for the creamer and sugar or the pitcher.

I am compelled to point out that a big variance is apparent in the size of the bowls which were made by turning up the edges of the square or round plates while they were still hot from the mold. Since this work was done by hand, sizes are rather imprecise on the factory listing and I have taken the liberty of listing the size I measured the bowl pictured to be. Bowls are often purchased by people who "just want a pretty piece of Depression Glass".

This is one of those patterns you will possible have to hassle over to convince some owner that what he has is not "Carnival Glass", "Vaseline Glass" or even older "Pattern" glass just because it may have color or similarities to all of the above.

	Crystal*, Pink Green, Amber	Other Colors		Crystal*, Pink Green, Amber	Other Colors
Bowl, 4½", 2 Handled Jelly	5.00	11.00	Bowl, 7½", Round, Plain Edge	7.00	12.00
**Bowl, 4½", Round, Lily	8.00	13.50	Bowl, 8¼", Celery	8.50	12.50
Bowl, 5½", Square	5.00	6.50	Creamer	8.50	15.00
Bowl, 5½", Blue, One Handle	6.00	8.00	Pitcher, 5¼", Pint Jug	97.50	
Bowl, 6", Deep Round	8.00	12.00	Plate, 7¾", Square	4.50	7.25
Bowl, 6¼" Round	6.00	12.00	Plate, 8¾", Round	5.00	9.50
Bowl, 6½" Round	6.00	12.50	Stemmed Jelly, 4½"	6.50	12.50
Bowl, 6½", 2 Handled Pickle	9.50	13.50	Stemmed Jelly, 4½", Flared		
Bowl, 6¾", Round, Unflared	8.25	11.00	Top	8.00	15.00
Bowl, 7¼", Round, Flared	7.50	13.50	Sugar	8.50	15.00
Bowl, 7½", Round, Fluted			Vase, 6", Bouquet	7.50	15.00
Edges	16.50	17.50			

"BOWKNOT"   UNKNOWN MANUFACTURER Probably late 1920's

Color: Green.

When my wife saw the pattern shots for Bow Knot for the first time she exclaimed, "What a darling pattern! I'd like to collect that!" I told her she'd have a hard time finding enough to serve guests as there were only seven pieces known then. That was 1970. Little did I know those same seven pieces would still be all that was known a decade later! Surely the cup had a saucer, or a punch bowl, at one time; and in an era when pitcher use was so common place, it seems plausible to me that the two tumblers demanded a pitcher.

From time to time I run into flurries of excitement that a sugar and creamer have been discovered; but invariably these turn out to be Fostoria's "June" pattern which has a similar bow etched into the glass rather than having the design molded into the glass as this pattern design is. Too, the Fostoria glassware is thinner and of better quality. These sugar and creamers are usually blue or yellow further identifying them as Fostoria. To date, only the green "Bowknot" has appeared in Depression circles.

Wouldn't it be a treat if you could find an undiscovered piece!

	Green		Green
Bowl, 4½" Berry	2.75	Sherbet, Low Footed	3.50
Bowl, 5½" Cereal	4.75	Tumbler, 5", 10 oz.	8.50
Cup	3.50	Tumbler, 5", 10 oz. Footed	8.50
Plate, 7" Salad	3.00		

*All pices except pitcher, 25% to 40% lower.
**Red: $45.00.

Please refer to Foreword for pricing information

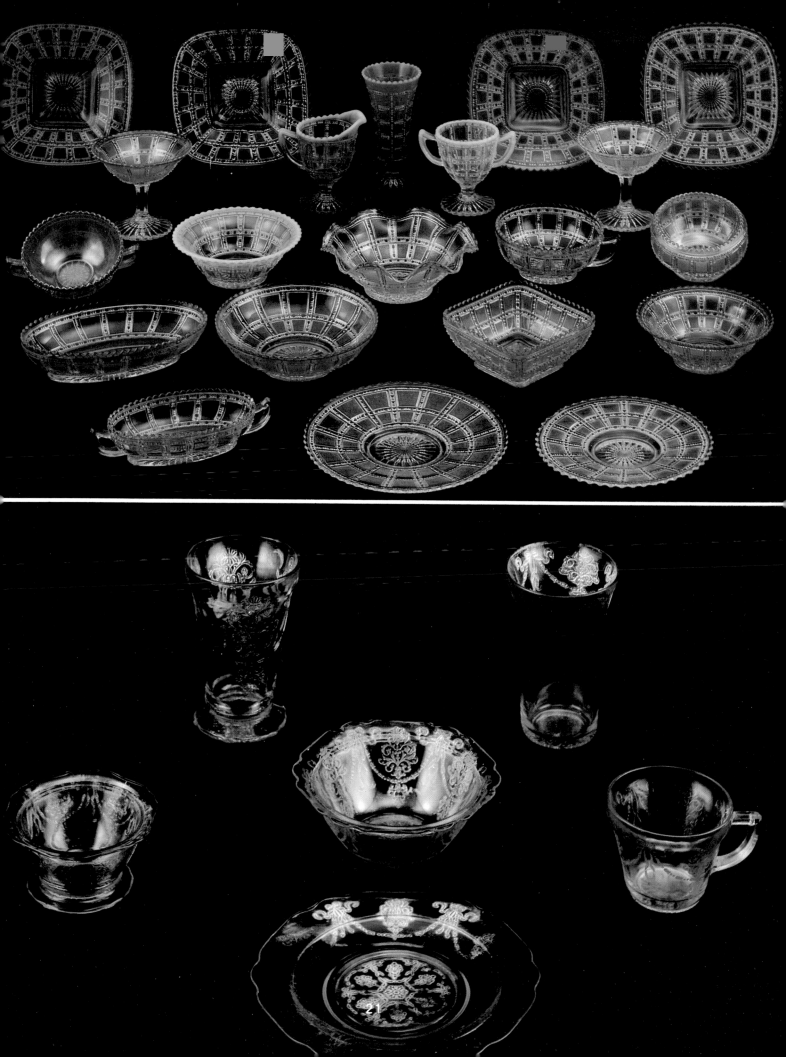

BLOCK OPTIC, "BLOCK" HOCKING GLASS COMPANY 1929-1933

Colors: Green, pink, yellow, crystal.

Many companies made block-like patterns during the Depression era, often making Block Optic difficult for newcomers to the field to recognize. A couple of helps, beside the picture and listing of pieces, are knowing that a number of the Block Optic pieces Hocking made have shapes similar to Hocking's Cameo pattern; and knowing that most of the stemmed pieces have rayed bottoms.

Horrors! An invaluable word was omitted from a sentence in the third edition book and did I get letters---and saucers---through the mail for confirmation! The sentence should have read that "one major note is that the YELLOW saucer and sherbet plate are the same". Unfortunately, "Yellow" was left out. A couple of reliable dealers have since told me that they've even seen the ring in yellow saucers; so the whole issue is academic at this point! However, I have shown BOTH (types) Block saucers as pattern shots this time; and in the picture you are shown all four cup styles! The two cups on the left use the 5¾" saucer; the two on the right belong to the 6 1/8" saucer. Still, however, many cups were sold and are still found on sherbet plates.

The decorated tumble-up was labeled as an Art Deco piece. The paint is quite chipped and flaked all these years later and unless someone out there is wild about it I'm stripping it off! I thought it might be interesting to photograph it first.

Green commands the most attention and the bigger prices; yet Block Optic still remains a pattern for beginning collectors to consider. There have been price jumps recently in dinner plates, the squatty, flat shakers and goblets in all sizes.

Crystal, when it shows up, commands half the price of green and pink.

	Pink, Green	Yellow		Pink, Green	Yellow
Bowl, 4¼" Berry	3.00		Plate, 9" Dinner	9.00	10.00
Bowl, 5¼" Cereal	4.50	5.00	Plate, 9" Grill	6.50	
Bowl, 7" Salad	7.50	9.50	Plate, 10¼" Sandwich	10.00	
Bowl, 8½" Large Berry	9.50	12.50	Salt and Pepper, Footed	17.50	49.50
Butter Dish and Cover, 3" x 5"	22.50		Salt and Pepper, Squatty	20.00	
Candlesticks, 1¾", Pr.	17.50		Sandwich Server, Center Handle	17.50	
Candy Jar and Cover, 2¼"	17.50	35.00	Saucer 5¾"	3.00	
Candy Jar Cover, 6¼"	25.00		Saucer 6 1/8"	3.00	7.50
Comport, 4" Wide Mayonnaise	8.50		Sherbet, Non Stemmed	3.00	
Creamer, Three Styles: Cone			Sherbet, 3¼", 5½ oz.	4.00	6.50
Shaped, Round Footed and			Sherbet, 4¾", 6 oz.	7.50	9.50
Flat	6.00	7.50	Sugar, Three Styles: As Creamer	7.50	7.50
Cup, Four Styles	3.00	4.00	Tumbler, 3½", 5 oz. Flat	9.00	
Goblet, 4" Cocktail	9.50		Tumbler, 4", 5 oz. Footed	6.50	
Goblet, 4½", Wine	9.50		Tumbler, 9 oz. Flat	6.50	
Goblet, 5¾", 9 oz.	9.00		Tumbler, 9 oz. Footed	9.00	9.00
Goblet, 7¼", Thin 9 oz.	15.00	13.50	Tumbler, 10 oz. Flat	9.00	
Ice Tub or Butter Tub, Open	15.00		Tumbler, 6", 10 oz. Footed	9.50	12.50
Mug, Flat Creamer, No Spout	22.50		Tumble-up Night Set: 3" Tumbler		
Pitcher, 8½", 54 oz.	20.00		Bottle and Tumbler, 6" High	30.00	
Pitcher, 8", 80 oz.	25.00		Vase, 5¾", Blown	57.50	
Plate, 6" Sherbet	1.50	2.00	Whiskey, 2½"	6.50	
Plate, 8" Luncheon	2.50	3.50			

"BUBBLE", "BULLSEYE", "PROVINCIAL"
ANCHOR HOCKING GLASS COMPANY 1934-1965

Colors: Pink, light blue, dark green, red, crystal.

This pattern has a "lineage" as it were. It's first ancestor was a pink bowl named "Bullseye" in 1934; then, in the 1940's its pale blue off-spring was called "Fire King"; much later, in the mid 1960's Royal Ruby was produced under the name "Provincial". Depression devotees have called them all "Bubble" and that's the name that has stuck.

For a long time, this pattern was sneered at by advanced collectors; it was the "country cousin" which was seldom noticed. However, this is rapidly changing. Dealers who previously laughed about leaving stacks of it behind in a shop have now returned to grab it up, sadly finding in some instances that someone has beaten them there. Granted, most collectors are buying the light blue since crystal still has few advocates.

Creamers, soup bowls, platters and even grill plates in blue are fast becoming extinct.

Several pieces of pink, aside from the ever present 8 3/8" berry bowl (Bullseye), have surfaced. These include a cup and saucer and a small bowl, presumably the individual bowl for the larger berry (I haven't a picture yet to confirm its actual size).

Candlesticks have only been found in dark green and crystal thus far, although I have unconfirmed reports of one in black. Have you seen any other colors?

The most unusual piece to surface to date is that flange edged bowl which is shown here as a pattern shot! This one came from Ohio. Keep looking; there are probably others.

Odd colors such as amber, iridized crystal, fired on pink similar to that found in Oyster and Pearl pattern, and even an opaque green have turned up in this pattern. These pieces tend to be more interesting than valuable.

This pattern should be quite durable since the 1942 Anchor Hocking ad guaranteed this "Fire-King" tableware to be "heat-proof", indeed a "tableware that can be used in the oven, on the table, in the refrigerator". Presumably since the ad is dated 1942, they're referring solely to the light blue color. This added dimension is unique to this pattern as most Depression Glass will not stand up to quick changes from hot to cold. I learned this the hard way by serving piping hot broccoli onto a cold Dogwood grill plate! It cracked beautifully down the center from side to side.

	Dark Green	Light Blue	Ruby Red		Dark Green	Light Blue	Ruby Red
Bowl, 4" Berry	1.50	4.00		Plate, 6¾" Bread and			
Bowl, 4½" Fruit	1.50	3.00	2.25	Butter	1.00	1.50	
Bowl, 5¼" Cereal	2.00	4.00		Plate, 9 3/8" Grill		4.50	
Bowl, 7¾" Flat Soup		4.50		Plate, 9 3/8" Dinner	4.00	4.50	4.50
Bowl, 8 3/8" Large Berry				Platter, 12" Oval		6.50	
(Pink—$2.50)	4.50	6.00		***Saucer	1.00	2.50	2.00
Candlesticks (Crystal -				Sugar	4.50	6.00	
$10.00 Pr.)	15.00			Tidbit (2 Tier)			12.00
Creamer	4.50	12.50		Tumbler, 6 oz. Juice			5.00
*Cup	1.50	2.50	3.00	Tumbler, 9 oz. Water			4.50
Lamp, 2 Styles, Crystal Only - 17.50				Tumbler, 12 oz. Iced Tea			7.50
**Pitcher, 64 oz., Ice Lip			22.50	Tumbler, 16 oz.			
				Lemonade			12.00

*Pink — $25.00.
**Crystal — $20.00.
***Pink — $15.00.

Please refer to Foreword for pricing information

CAMEO, "BALLERINA" or "DANCING GIRL"

HOCKING GLASS COMPANY 1930-1934

Colors: Green, yellow, pink and crystal with platinum rim.

The collector of Cameo who already has a nearly completed set can utter a sigh of relief when he looks at some of today's prices! Bowls, dinner plates and other basic pieces have taken a dramatic price hike; the more exotic pieces have only increased moderately.

In pink, two more ice tubs have now surfaced; and in yellow, a poorly molded, weak patterned syrup pitcher has shown up! I guess there's hope for a pink pitcher yet! I would emphasize that a pitcher having Cameo shape isn't considered to be Cameo; it has to have the design on it.

In the past, the 5¼", 15 oz. flat tumbler has been omitted from my list, though I can't figure why since this is shown in the catalogues as far back as 1930! One of those mysterious oversights that occur. Sorry! Incidentally, the water bottle, listed as a decanter, is shown in the 1931 catalogue without the stopper. This explains, does it not, why there are so many stopperless bottles around?

In a seven week period, five center handled servers surfaced! Unreal! I had one of them photographed; unfortunately, that was one of the first set of pictures for this book that mysteriously lost themselves at the publishers, no less!

The only reason I can see for the Cameo saucer not getting any higher is that a collector will only pay so much for a saucer! It is truly a rare saucer since most cups reside on sherbet plate substitutes. The saucer with the cup ring is pictured in pink.

Pink and crystal drip trays continue to appear sans indent for the cream pitcher. For the new initiates, the domino drip tray was called that because (Domino brand?) sugar cubes set around the cream pitcher which rested within the ring.

A late find is a footed green piece that may be a lamp base since it has a "3" molded into the side which may indicate a No. "3" burner fits.

	Green	Yellow	Pink	Crys/ Plat
Bowl, 4¼" Sauce				4.00
Bowl, 4¾" Cream Soup	32.50			
Bowl, 5½" Cereal	9.50	11.50		3.00
Bowl, 7¼" Salad	18.50			
Bowl, 8¼" Large Berry	20.00	27.50		
Bowl, 9" Rimmed Soup	17.50			
Bowl, 10" Oval Vegetable	9.50	15.00		
Bowl, 11" 3 Leg Console	22.50	42.50	15.00	
Butter Dish and Cover	97.50	500.00		
Cake Plate, 10" 3 Legs	10.00			
Candlesticks, 4" Pr.	42.50			
Candy Jar, Low 4" and Cover	30.00	40.00	250.00	
Candy Jar, 6½" Tall and Cover	67.50	225.00		
Cocktail Shaker (Metal Lid) Appears in Crystal Only				150.00
Comport, 5" Wide, Mayonnaise	13.50			
Cookie Jar and Cover	22.50			
Creamer, 3¼"	10.00	7.50		
Creamer, 4¼"	8.50		42.50	
Cup, Two Styles	6.00	4.50	42.50	
Decanter, 10" With Stopper	52.50			

Cameo Prices Continued On Page 28.

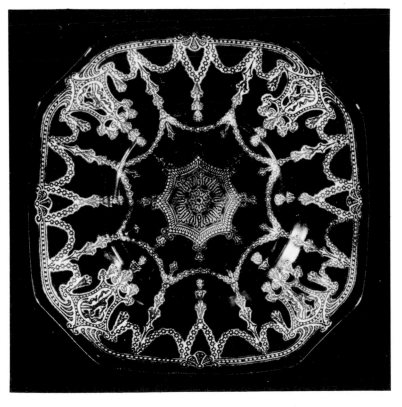

CAMEO, "BALLERINA" or "DANCING GIRL" (Con't.)

	Green	Yellow	Pink	Crys/ Plat
Decanter, 10" With Stopper, Frosted (Stoppers Represent ½ Value of Decanter)	22.50			
Domino Tray, 7" With 3" Indentation	42.50			
Domino Tray, 7" With No Indentation			135.00	80.00
Goblet, 3½" Wine	75.00			
Goblet, 4" Wine	35.00		150.00	
Goblet, 6" Water	22.50		75.00	
Ice Bowl or Open Butter 3" Tall x 5½" Wide	77.50		325.00	150.00
Jam Jar, 2" and Cover	62.50			75.00
Pitcher, 5¾" Syrup or Milk, 20 oz.	107.50	150.00		
Pitcher, 6" Juice, 36 oz.	25.00			
Pitcher, 8½" Water, 56 oz.	22.50			
Plate, 6" Sherbet	2.50	1.75	35.00	1.75
Plate, 7" Salad				3.00
Plate, 8" Luncheon	4.50	2.25	22.50	3.50
Plate, 8½" Square	15.00	45.00		
Plate, 9½" Dinner	9.50	5.00	30.00	
Plate, 10" Sandwich	6.00		30.00	
Plate, 10½" Grill	6.50	6.00	32.50	
Plate, 10½" Grill With Closed Handles	7.00	5.75		
Plate, 11½" With Closed Handles	6.00	5.00		
Platter, 12", Closed Handles	10.00	13.50		
Relish, 3 Part, 7½" Footed	9.00	47.50		
Salt and Pepper, Footed, Pr.	35.00		450.00	
Sandwich Server, Center Handle	850.00			
Saucer With Cup Ring	32.50			
Saucer 6" (Sherbet Plate)	2.50	1.75	35.00	
Sherbet, 3 1/8"	7.00	15.00	25.00	
Sherbet, 4 7/8"	17.50	19.50	47.50	
Sugar, 3¼"	7.50	7.50		
Sugar, 4¼"	7.50		42.50	
Tumbler, 3¾", 5 oz. Juice	14.00		55.00	
Tumbler, 4", 9 oz. Water	12.50		55.00	7.50
Tumbler, 4¾", 10 oz. Flat	12.50			
Tumbler, 5", 11 oz. Flat	15.00	22.50	67.50	
Tumbler, 5¼" 15 oz.	23.50			
Tumbler, 3 oz. Footed, Juice	32.50		77.50	
Tumbler, 5", 9 oz. Footed	12.50	10.00	72.50	
Tumbler, 5¾", 11 oz. Footed	22.50			
Tumbler, 6 3/8", 15 oz. Footed	125.00			
Vase, 5¾"	75.00			
Vase, 8"	15.00			
Water Bottle (Dark Green) Whitehouse Vinegar	17.50			

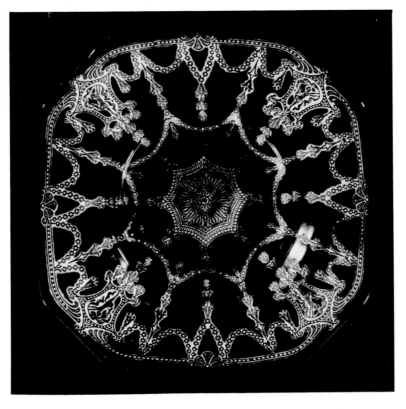

29

CHERRY BLOSSOM   JEANNETTE GLASS COMPANY 1930-1939

Colors: Pink, green, delphite (opaque blue), crystal, jadite (opaque green), red.

(See Reproduction Section)

Cherry Blossom is one of the top five most collected patterns in Depression Glass. It is plentiful, easily recognized and attractive. It is further distinguished by having a number of very rarely found pieces in its repertoire: a 9″ oval platter on which the creamer and sugar reside; a divided, orange/pink relish tray, patterned after the two handled, round 10½″ sandwich tray; pink cherry shakers of which only two original sets are known; a pink cherry cookie jar; a translucent apple green colored plate; an amber child's cup and saucer; an ice blue cherry bowl; and a transparent red dinner plate, bowl, cup and footed all-over-pattern tumbler. All of these oddities conspire to add zest to the collecting of this pattern. You feel that just around the corner MIGHT be another rare Cherry Blossom item.

All these reasons unfortunately, make this pattern a prime target for the reproduction artisan. First of the "new" pieces to appear was a child's cup with a slightly lop-sided handle and the cherries hanging upside down when the cup was held in the right hand. (This was due to the inversion of the design when the mold, taken from the original cup, was inverted to create the outside of the "new" cup). This oddity was soon corrected, however, by re-inverting the inverted mold. There were also saucers with slightly off center designs. Next came the "child's" butter dish which was not made at all in the original child's set. It was essentially the child's cup (sans handle) turned upside down over the saucer with a little knob added for lifting purposes. You could get this in pink, green, light blue, cobalt, gray-green and iridescent carnival colors.

Lately, and more disturbing, have come butter dishes and shakers which you may **see pictured in the section on reproductions at the back.** At this writing, there are reports of new Cherry Blossom pitcher and tumbler sets in the making. If I can, before this book goes to press, I'll try to have them pictured; if not, then be aware they may appear! These are the scalloped AOP pitcher and tumbler.

Thus far, reproductions are readily recognizable to experts in the field; there are always telltale signs. But the less than expert need to keep up with what is being reproduced by subscribing to one of the trade publications that keep you in touch monthly with what is happening. This will keep you out of the hands of the unscrupulous. My second rule of thumb is simply not to pay an outlandish sum of money for a piece of Depression Glass unless you know what you're doing!

Happily, reproductions represent only a minute particle in the over all picture of Depression Glass; they're a slight nuisance which must be kept track of. Unhappily, for Cherry Blossom collectors, their pattern is very popular and hence there is a ready market for the reproducers.

Quite a few items have inflated in value since the third book. Among those are the cereal bowl, the soup and the 9″ platter, particularly in pink. There have been several reports of a 9″ platter in green; but all have turned out to be 11″ instead. The platter is measured outside edge to outside edge, not inside rim to inside rim which makes a two inch difference.

A bargain in today's Depression Glass world is delphite Cherry Blossom. Many pieces are selling for the same prices as in 1971. Inflation alone should have doubled the price by now; and not all of the pieces are hard to find. The flat, two handled sandwich and the two handled bowl, in fact, are rather common.

At this writing, pink and green tumblers have almost tripled in price as compared with the delphite. Due to a greater and greater number of collectors turning to pink Cherry Blossom, many prices in pink are priced above their counterparts in green. Demand and scarcity of an item are the two factors which determine price; and often, demand outweighs scarcity. Some items can be so rare that they are, in effect, uncollectible! This usually happens in a lesser known pattern. Rare Cherry Blossom pieces should have value simply because there are thousands of persons collecting the pattern.

The letters AOP in the price listing refer to pieces having an "all over pattern"; PAT means "pattern at the top" only.

See Page 32 For Prices.

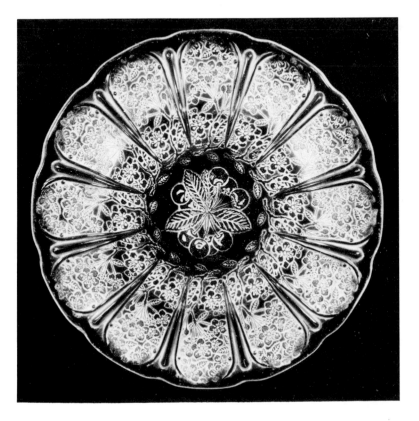

CHERRY BLOSSOM (Con't.)

	Pink	Green	Delphite	Jadite
Bowl, 4¾" Berry	6.50	7.50	8.50	
Bowl, 5¾" Cereal	14.50	16.00		
Bowl, 7¾" Flat Soup	26.50	30.00		
*Bowl, 8½" Round Berry	10.50	12.50	37.50	
Bowl, 9" Oval Vegetable	10.00	15.00	40.00	
Bowl, 9" 2 Handled	10.00	12.50	12.00	250.00
Bowl, 10½", 3 Leg Fruit	22.50	27.50		250.00
Butter Dish and Cover	57.50	67.50		
Cake Plate (3 Legs) 10¼"	11.50	14.50		
Coaster	6.50	7.50		
Creamer	8.00	10.00	15.50	
Cup	10.00	11.00		
Mug, 7 oz.	90.00	97.50		
Pitcher 6¾" AOP, 36 oz. Scalloped or Round Bottom	25.00	32.50		
Pitcher, 8" PAT, 42 oz. Flat	22.50	24.50		
Pitcher, 8" PAT, 36 oz. Footed	25.00	37.50	89.50	
Plate, 6" Sherbet	3.25	3.50	8.50 (design on top)	
Plate, 7" Salad	9.50	10.00		
**Plate, 9" Dinner	9.00	11.00	10.50	
Plate, 9" Grill	8.00	10.00		
Plate, 10" Grill		32.50		
Platter, 9" Oval	475.00			
Platter, 11" Oval	14.00	17.50	29.50	
Platter, 13" and 13" Divided	22.50	29.50		
Salt and Pepper (Scalloped Bottom)	750.00	550.00		
Saucer	3.50	3.50	4.25	
Sherbet	8.00	9.50	10.00	
Sugar	6.50	7.50	15.50	
Sugar Cover	6.00	9.00		
Tray, 10½" Sandwich	11.00	12.50	13.00	
Tumbler, 3¾", 4 oz. Footed, AOP, Round or Scalloped	10.00	13.50	16.00	
Tumbler, 4½", 9 oz. Round Foot AOP	20.00	23.50	16.50	
***Tumbler, 4½", 8 oz. Scalloped Foot AOP	20.00	23.50	16.50	
Tumbler, 3½", 4 oz. Flat PAT	8.50	10.00		
Tumbler, 4¼", 9 oz. Flat PAT	10.00	12.50		
Tumbler, 5", 12 oz. Flat PAT	20.00	22.50		

*Yellow — $325.00.   Red — $325.00.
**Translucent Green, Red — $150.00
***Red — $150.00

Cherry Blossom — Child's Junior Dinner Set

	Pink	Delphite
Creamer	18.50	21.50
Sugar	18.50	21.50
Plate, 6"	7.25	8.25 (design on bottom)
Cup	13.00	20.00
Saucer	4.00	4.50
14 Piece Set	127.50	167.50

Original box sells for $7.50 extra with these sets.

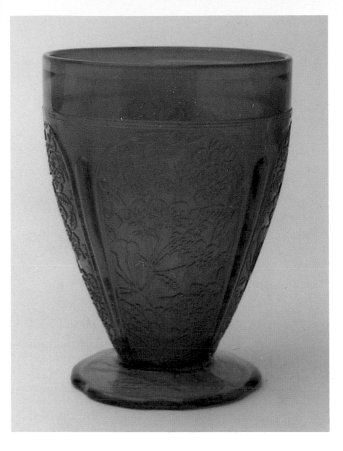

33

CHINEX CLASSIC

MACBETH-EVANS DIVISION OF CORNING GLASS WORKS Late 1930 - Early 1940

Colors: Ivory, ivory decal decorated.

Scarcity of Chinex has relegated this to a minor pattern. It's hard to become interested in something you seldom see. For a while, prices for this pattern shot up due to its scarcity; but with so few people asking for it, prices have leveled off now.

Chinex with the scroll-like design in the pattern (which distinguishes it from the plainer designed Cremax discussed later) is easier to find than the decal decorated pieces. I'm told they make excellent everyday dishes; several collectors tell me they feel they're superior to Corning's modern day line, particularly in price. One major drawback, of course, is that if it gets broken you can't get a replacement guarantee as with the newer line.

There are several different fired under the glaze decals to be found in this pattern, the most popular one being the brown castle design. Unfortunately, the brown castle design is the hardest to locate, though the shaded items run a close second.

Sherbets and soup bowls are seldom found in Chinex and the butter dish is the most valuable piece. Even people who don't pretend to collect the pattern seek the butter dish to sell or trade.

The Chinex scroll design is found only on the lid of the butter dish and not on the base. The base has a pie-crust type edge reminiscent of the Cremax pattern when found without the lid.

	Browntone or Plain Ivory	Decal Decorated*
Bowl, 5¾" Cereal	3.25	4.00
Bowl, 7" Flat Soup	6.00	8.00
Bowl, 9" Vegetable	10.00	12.00
Butter Dish	47.50	62.50
Creamer	4.50	6.50
Cup	3.50	4.00
Plate, 6¼" Sherbet	2.00	2.00
Plate, 9¾" Dinner	3.50	4.50
Plate, 11½" Sandwich or Cake	7.00	7.50
Saucer	2.00	3.00
Sherbet, Low Footed	6.50	8.00
Sugar, Open	4.50	6.50

CIRCLE HOCKING GLASS COMPANY 1930's

Color: Green.

Circle was a smaller line of Hocking's. It is characterized by having bands of circles around the mid line of its pieces. You probably won't find a great deal of this around; but since it does turn up occasionally, I thought it might be fun to include it. I couldn't turn up a pitcher for the photograph. Maybe next time!

	Green		Green
Bowl, 4½"	2.00	Saucer	1.00
Creamer	3.50	Sherbet	2.75
Cup	2.50	Sugar	3.50
Decanter, Handled	15.00	Tumbler, 4 oz. Juice	3.00
Goblet, 4½" Wine	6.50	Tumbler, 8 oz. Water	3.50
Pitcher, 80 oz.	13.50	Vase, Hat Shape	12.50
Plate, 6" Sherbet	1.25		

*Castle decal about 20% higher in most areas.

Please refer to Foreword for pricing information

35

CLOVERLEAF HAZEL ATLAS GLASS COMPANY 1930-1936

Colors: Pink, green, yellow, crystal, black

Cloverleaf pattern has nearly disappeared from the market. People who collect black can still find basic luncheon pieces, i.e. cup, saucer, luncheon plates and sugars and creamers; but other pieces seem practically nonexistent, a large factor in pricing said pieces, of course.

Yellow 5", 7" and deep 8" bowls are fast disappearing.

The larger ash tray in black is turning out to be the more rare of the two though it was the first to be discovered.

New collectors should note that the sherbet plate has the design in the center; the saucer does not have the design; yet both items are the same size.

Cloverleaf is a whimsically attractive pattern which I am certain would attract more collectors if it were in plentiful supply.

	Pink Green	Yellow	Black
Ash Tray 4", Match Holder in Center			35.00
Ash Tray 5¾", Match Holder in Center			57.50
Bowl, 4" Dessert	5.00	10.00	
Bowl, 5" Cereal	7.50	12.50	
Bowl, 7" Salad, Deep	12.00	25.00	
Candy Dish and Cover	*25.00	79.50	
Creamer, Footed, 3 5/8"	6.00	8.00	8.00
Cup	3.50	5.00	6.00
Plate, 6" Sherbet	2.00	3.50	16.50
Plate, 8" Luncheon	3.50	8.00	7.50
Plate, 10¼" Grill	5.50	9.00	
Salt and Pepper, Pair	*17.50	77.50	45.00
Saucer	1.50	2.50	2.50
Sherbet, 3" Footed	3.75	6.50	9.75
Sugar, Footed, 3 5/8"	5.50	7.50	7.50
Tumbler, 4", 9 oz. Flat	11.50		
Tumbler, 3¾", 10 oz. Flat	12.00		
Tumbler, 5¾", 10 oz. Footed	12.00	15.00	

Design highlighted in photographs to emphasize pattern.

*Green only.

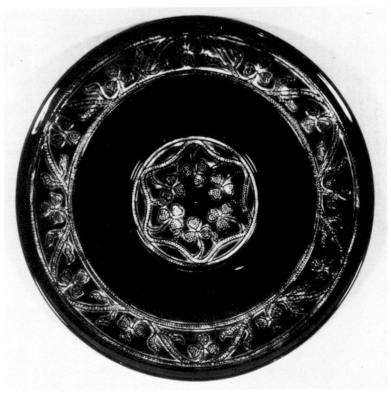

37

COLONIAL, "KNIFE AND FORK" HOCKING GLASS COMPANY 1934-1936

Colors: Pink, green, crystal, opaque white

Colonial pattern has a timeless elegance in its simplistic design, and it sets a beautiful table, particularly when some of the stemware is used. However, unless you have unlimited funds, I would suggest that you choose a particular stemware to collect rather than trying to obtain them all as they are numerous in this pattern.

Colonial is distinctive in that it features a cheese board server which both butter and cheese top fit. The cheese top, however, is about half an inch shorter than the butter top.

There appear to be more butter tops than bottoms. This may be due to the weight of the top as it's quite heavy. Most butter dish bottoms you do run into are chunked rather than just mildly chipped.

I mentioned in my third edition that I hadn't seen pink cream soups and thereafter it seemed to "rain" them. Everywhere I went there were two or three. (If I thought that technique would work with some of this other glass that is seemingly non existent. . .!) Anyway, the cream soups in pink all have ground bottoms, usually a characteristic of better grade glassware than our Depression Glass; so that made an interesting twist to their appearance.

Cereal bowls (5″) in both pink and green remain in hiding. Several collectors I know have been looking for two or three years for these little gems to add to their set.

Newly discovered are pink and green mugs in this pattern, two green and about twelve pink to be exact. One of the pink is pictured.

Price of spooners has climbed drastically. Beginners should know that the spooner is taller than the sugar and therefore the handles sit farther away from the base than do those of the sugar. (Sometimes one runs into a lidless sugar and it's difficult to tell which is what).

Tumblers, low soups and even dinner plates in green are getting extremely difficult to find.

Notice the lone beaded top pink pitcher pictured on the cover which I mentioned in the last book. This is an uncommon find.

There is a white, Colonial-like plate, cup and saucer floating about. However, due to the concentric rings on the plate similar to those of Chinex, I'm prone to think it might have been produced by Corning Glassworks. Should you find validation pro or con, I'd be delighted to hear from you.

The very latest find is a 4″, 9 oz. water tumbler in Royal Ruby.

	Pink	Green		Pink	Green
Bowl, 4½″ Berry	4.00	5.50	Plate, 6″ Sherbet	2.00	2.50
Bowl, 5½″ Cereal	12.50	22.50	Plate, 8½″ Luncheon	2.75	3.50
Bowl, 4½″ Cream Soup	17.50	17.50	Plate, 10″ Dinner	12.50	18.50
Bowl, 7″ Low Soup	15.00	25.00	Plate, 10″ Grill	5.00	8.50
Bowl, 9″ Large Berry	9.00	10.50	Platter, 12″ Oval	8.50	10.00
Bowl, 10″ Oval Vegetable	10.00	13.50	Salt and Pepper, Pair	92.50	95.00
Butter Dish and Cover	360.00	35.00	Saucer (White 3.00) (Same as		
Cheese Dish (as shown)		67.50	sherbet plate)	2.00	2.50
Creamer, 5″, 8 oz. (Milk			Sherbet	5.00	7.50
Pitcher)	9.00	12.50	Spoon Holder or Celery	50.00	57.50
Cup (White 7.00)	3.50	5.00	Sugar, 5″	8.50	9.00
Goblet, 3¾″, 1 oz. Cordial		17.50	Sugar Cover	12.50	9.50
Goblet, 4″, 3 oz. Cocktail	12.50	15.00	Tumbler, 3″, 5 oz. Juice	7.00	10.00
Goblet, 4½″, 2½ oz. Wine	12.50	15.00	Tumbler, 4″, 9 oz. Water	6.50	11.00
Goblet, 5¼″, 4 oz. Claret	13.00	13.50	Tumbler, 10 oz.	10.00	15.00
Goblet, 5¾″, 8½ oz. Water	12.50	15.00	Tumbler, 12 oz. Iced Tea	14.50	22.50
Mug, 4½″ 12 oz.	75.00	100.00	Tumbler, 15 oz. Lemonade	17.50	29.50
Pitcher, 7″, 54 oz. Ice Lip or			Tumbler, 3¼″, 3 oz. Footed	7.50	9.50
None	27.50	25.50	Tumbler, 4″, 5 oz. Footed	9.50	11.50
*Pitcher, 7¾″, 68 oz. Ice Lip or			Tumbler, 5¼″, 10 oz. Ftd.	10.00	13.50
None	30.00	42.50	Whiskey, 2½″, 1½ oz.	6.00	7.50

*Beaded top in pink $175.00

Please refer to Foreword for pricing information

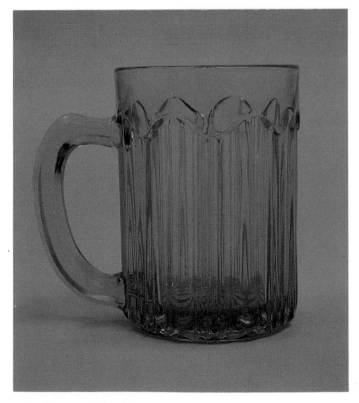

COLONIAL FLUTED, "ROPE" FEDERAL GLASS COMPANY 1928-1933

Colors: Green, crystal.

Colonial Fluted is collected by a few persons, but it is not one of the more popular patterns. This isn't because it is unattractive. It is due to its being in very scarce supply and to the fact that the pieces found are scuffed and scratched, a condition few collectors are likely to overlook.

A dinner plate and some other pieces have turned up with the rope-like design around the rim; but lacking the panels. The "F" in the shield marking of this particular company identifies it as having been made by the same manufacturer, but whether the pieces were meant to be part of the same pattern remains a mystery at present. I tend to think not. However, as there are so few pieces to this pattern to be had, if you find it and if it mixes well with the pattern, why not use it?

There is a bridge set in crystal that is a worthy find whether you are a collector of Colonial Fluted or not. Usually the decals of hearts, diamonds, clubs and spades are quite worn in the set.

	Green		Green
Bowl, 4" Berry	1.50	Plate, 6" Sherbet	1.00
Bowl, 6" Cereal	2.00	Plate, 8" Luncheon	2.25
Bowl, 6½" Deep Salad	5.50	Saucer	1.00
Bowl, 7½" Large Berry	6.00	Sherbet	3.50
Creamer	3.50	Sugar	2.50
Cup	2.00	Sugar Cover	6.00

COLUMBIA FEDERAL GLASS COMPANY 1938-1942

Colors: Crystal, pink.

Columbia has been a much overlooked pattern in the past and I am happy to notice a trend to change this. This is one of the most attractive patterns to be had in crystal; and crystal Columbia is plentiful.

This pattern is rather unusual in that you will find the butter top in a number of flashed on colors: blue, iridescent, red, purple, amethyst and green. There may even be others; so you have a variety of decorative possibilities.

Finding pink Columbia will be a challenge. It's there, but not so often as the crystal; and dealers and collectors alike would beat a path to your door if you could turn up a butter dish in the pink Columbia pattern.

The only items to have made significant jumps in price have been the 5" cereal bowl and the 8" low soup. This is one of the patterns that can still be collected quickly and at under inflation prices. Too, it sets any table with a certain jeweled brilliance.

	Crystal		Crystal	Pink
Bowl, 5" Cereal	4.50	Cup	2.50	6.50
Bowl, 8" Low Soup	4.50	Plate, 6" Bread & Butter	1.00	3.00
Bowl, 8½" Salad	6.50	Plate, 9½" Luncheon	2.50	9.50
Bowl, 10½" Ruffled Edge	9.00	Plate, 11¾" Chop	5.50	
Butter Dish and Cover	15.00	Saucer	1.00	4.00
Ruby Flashed (17.50)		Snack Plate	4.00	
Other Flashed (16.00)				

CORONATION, "BANDED FINE RIB", "SAXON"

HOCKING GLASS COMPANY 1936-1940

Colors: Pink, crystal, royal ruby.

Coronation pattern has generated little interest in Depression circles, other than consternation. People are continually shipped a Coronation tumbler in place of a much rarer Lace Edge. It would make little difference in looks; but there is a difference in price! The more plentiful Coronation tumbler has fine rays going almost to the top of the glass whereas the rays of the Lace Edge tumbler do not.

Perhaps one reason so few people become interested in Coronation is because it has so few pieces to collect!

Pink and crystal pieces were made in 1936; red was made in 1940 during Anchor Hocking's Royal Ruby promotion. They evidently made an abundance of Royal Ruby berry sets as they tend to be rather common!

I would like to point out that the red coronation cup has no red saucer. It was promoted on a crystal saucer. However, I've heard of some people refusing to buy these sets as they weren't on a red saucer. Don't pass up an attractive Christmas or Valentine coffee set on that account! That's the way they came!

	Pink	Ruby Red		Pink	Ruby Red
Bowl, 4¼" Berry	1.50	4.00	Plate, 8½" Luncheon	2.50	4.00
Bowl, 6½" Nappy	2.50	6.50	Saucer (Same as 6" plate)	1.00	
Bowl, 8" Large Berry	5.00	9.50	Sherbet	2.50	3.50
Cup	2.50	3.00	Tumbler, 5",10 oz. Footed	6.50	
Plate, 6" Sherbet	1.00				

CREMAX

MACBETH-EVANS DIVISION OF CORNING GLASS WORKS Late 1930's - Early 1940's

Color: Cremax.

The popularity Cremax enjoyed a few years ago has faded from sight. In fact, this is one of the few patterns in Depression Glass that has actually dropped in price due to lack of demand. Perhaps now would be a good time to stock up since the supply of many other patterns is dwindling; that might make this one a "sleeper".

There is a tendency for some people to confuse Cremax and Chinex patterns. The basic difference is that Cremax doesn't have the scroll-like design of Chinex.

The word "cremax" will be used to describe an off-white color found in the American Sweetheart, Dogwood and Petalware patterns which were made by the Macbeth-Evans but not Corning. In the pattern Cremax, however, this distinction of color isn't relevant. Cremax pattern is mostly as white as Chinex pattern.

Cremax pattern hasn't any butter dish to date, though the one found in the Chinex pattern is often mistaken for a Cremax butter because of its pie-crust like edge to the bottom.

As with Chinex, the decals on these dishes are put on by the factory under the glaze; so there's no reason to worry they will come off easily.

	Cremax	Decal Decorated		Cremax	Decal Decorated
Bowl, 5¾" Cereal	2.50	3.50	Plate, 9¾" Dinner	3.00	4.50
Bowl, 9" Vegetable	5.00	6.50	Plate, 11½" Sandwich	4.50	6.50
Creamer	2.75	3.50	Saucer	1.25	1.25
Cup	2.50	3.25	Sugar, Open	2.75	3.50
Plate, 6¼" Bread and Butter	1.25	1.50			

Please refer to Foreword for pricing information

43

CUBE, "CUBIST" JEANNETTE GLASS COMPANY 1929-1933

Colors: Pink, green, crystal, ultra-marine.

The only reason I can figure for this pattern not skyrocketing in price along with some others is due to the lack of any dinner plates and the relative scarcity of the green.

You could still gather a luncheon set rather easily; but basic serving pieces and pitcher and tumblers are few and far between.

Only the salad bowl has turned up in the ultra-marine color. I keep thinking there must be some smaller bowls somewhere.

There are still few collectors of crystal Cube, a factor which holds the price down. Should you decide to collect the crystal, you should be forewarned that Fostoria Glass Company has a pattern called "American" that is very similar to Jeannette's Cube. However, as Fostoria's is a better quality glass, it has greater clarity than the older Cube and generally bespeaks better glassware. Fostoria's "American" isn't Depression Glass, however; Jeannette's "Cube" is!

	Pink	Green		Pink	Green
Bowl, 4½" Dessert	2.25	3.00	Plate, 8" Luncheon	2.00	3.00
Bowl, 4½" Deep	3.00	4.00	Powder Jar and Cover,		
*Bowl, 6½" Salad	5.00	6.75	3 Legs	9.50	12.50
Butter Dish and Cover	37.50	42.50	Salt and Pepper, Pr.	17.50	20.00
Candy Jar and Cover, 6½"	17.50	20.00	Saucer	1.25	1.75
Coaster, 3¼"	2.50	3.50	Sherbet, Footed	3.50	4.50
Creamer, 2"	2.00		Sugar, 2"	2.00	
Creamer, 3"	4.00	5.00	Sugar, 3"	2.50	4.00
Cup	3.00	4.00	Sugar/Candy Cover	5.00	6.00
Pitcher, 8¾", 45 oz.	67.50	97.50	Tray for 3" Creamer and		
Plate, 6" Sherbet	1.50	2.00	Sugar, 7½" (crystal only)	3.50	
			Tumbler, 4", 9 oz.	10.50	20.00

*Ultra-Marine — $27.50.

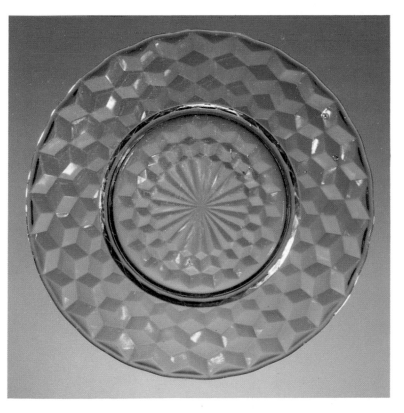

"CUPID" PADEN CITY GLASS COMPANY

Colors: Pink, green, light blue.

"Cupid" is another pattern I happened to find a large supply of at one time and therefore became interested in it. Unfortunately, since that one big windfall, finding additional pieces has been VERY slow.

Shapes for this pattern and the Peacock and Wild Rose shown later in the book are very similar. That isn't unusual since they were both manufactured by the same company.

I have only been able to find that beautiful shade of blue in the plate shown. It's too pretty for there not to have been more!

Notice the center handled bowls in which the handle actually gets in your way. This certainly limits what can be served in these---without sticking your finger into it, that is! Maybe that's where Cupid's arrows fit?

Don't be surprised if you find additional pieces or if you get "hooked" by the pattern. It seemed absolutely made for my "Valentine"; possibly yours would like it, too!

	Pink, Green & Blue
Bowl, 8½", Oval Ftd.	15.00
Bowl, 9¼", Ftd. Fruit	14.00
Bowl, 9¼", Center Handled	15.00
Bowl, 11", Console	14.00
Candlestick, 5" Wide, Pair	15.00
Comport, 6¼"	11.50
Creamer, 4½", Ftd.	10.00
Ice Bucket, 6"	25.00
Mayonnaise, 6" Diameter, Fits on 8" Plate	20.00
Plate, 10½"	12.50
Sugar, 4¼", Ftd.	10.00
Tray, 10½", Center Handled	12.50
Tray, 10 7/8", Oval, Ftd.	15.00
Vase, 8¼", Elliptical	25.00

"DAISY", NUMBER 620 INDIANA GLASS COMPANY

Colors: Crystal, 1933; amber, 1940; dark green and milk glass, 1960's.

The latterly issued dark green and milk glass colors were marketed by Indiana Glass Company under the name "Heritage"; due to their being twins to older glassware however, all issues are sold by Depression dealers under the name of "Daisy".

There are several pieces of "Daisy" that have all but disappeared from the market. These include the cereal bowls, the 12 oz. footed tumbler and the 9 3/8" deep berry bowl. Accordingly, you will note a particular jump in prices on these items. You may consider yourself fortunate if you have already purchased them!

There is still little demand for crystal Daisy although it is more truly Depression Glass than any of the other lines! Pieces are available in this with gold or platinum rims which lend the table setting a certain elegance. However, in crystal, the pattern is visible enough to stand alone without further enhancement. Give crystal Daisy a try; I think you'll really be enchanted with it!

	Crystal	Amber		Crystal	Amber
Bowl, 4½" Berry	1.00	2.00	Plate, 9 3/8" Dinner	2.50	4.00
Bowl, 4½" Cream Soup	3.00	5.50	Plate, 10 3/8" Grill	3.00	4.50
Bowl, 6" Cereal	5.00	9.00	Plate, 11½" Cake or		
Bowl, 7 3/8" Deep Berry	5.00	8.50	Sandwich	3.50	8.00
Bowl, 9 3/8" Deep Berry	6.00	10.50	Platter, 10¾"	5.00	9.00
Bowl, 10" Oval Vegetable	5.00	7.50	Relish Dish, 3 Part, 8 3/8"	4.00	7.50
Creamer, Footed	3.50	5.50	Saucer	1.00	1.25
Cup	1.75	3.25	Sherbet, Footed	2.25	4.50
Plate, 6" Sherbet	1.00	1.50	Sugar, Footed	3.50	4.50
Plate, 7 3/8" Salad	1.25	2.25	Tumbler, 9 oz. Footed	5.00	9.00
Plate, 8 3/8" Luncheon	1.50	3.00	Tumbler, 12 oz. Footed	6.00	13.50

DIANA FEDERAL GLASS COMPANY 1937-1941

Colors: Pink, amber, crystal.

Diana was the mythological goddess of the moon. Having recently witnessed the phenomenon of the eclipse of the sun, one is able to look at the pattern shot of the plate and transfer that aura to Diana. Possibly this design was inspired by a lunar eclipse.

At any rate, Diana is one of the many swirled patterns in Depression Glass that people tend to confuse with Swirl and Twisted Optic. "How do you tell the difference?" I'm asked. Look in the bottom. If the bottom is swirled also, then the piece is likely to be Diana.

Diana is not plentiful; yet there is enough still around to handle a few more collectors provided you don't choose amber color. Amber shakers and candy dishes are becoming dim memories. Some few lucky collectors have found them! The pink candy dish is almost as elusive.

That frosted bowl in the back of the picture is unusual. Since a complete set of frosted pink Diana has surfaced, we do know that Federal dipped some of this pattern into the camphoric acid vat at one time. Frosted items, while novel, generally fetch smaller prices than do the normal line. There is very little demand for it.

A pink demitasse cup and saucer set has been found with the wire rack, see the crystal one pictured.

Some few items with Diana characteristics can be found in green such as a sherbet and the ash tray/coaster pictured.

	Amber, Crystal, Pink****		Amber, Crystal, Pink****
*Ash Tray, 3½"	2.50	Plate, 5½" Child's	2.50
Bowl, 5" Cereal	2.50	Plate, 6" Bread and Butter	1.50
Bowl, 5½" Cream Soup	4.50	Plate, 9½" Dinner	4.00
Bowl, 9" Salad	6.50	Plate, 11¾" Sandwich	4.50
Bowl, 11" Console Fruit	6.00	Platter, 12" Oval	5.50
Bowl, 12" Scalloped Edge	7.50	***Salt and Pepper, Pr.	22.50
**Candy Jar and Cover, Round	12.50	Saucer	1.25
Coaster, 3½"	2.50	Sherbet	4.50
Creamer, Oval	3.50	Sugar, Open, Oval	3.50
Cup	3.00	Tumbler, 4 1/8", 9 oz.	8.50
Cup, Demi-tasse, 2 oz.		Junior Set: 6 Cups, Saucer	
and 4½" Saucer Set	4.00	and Plates with Round	
		Rack	35.00

*Green — $3.00
**Amber — $22.50
***Amber — $67.50
****Crystal 30% Less

Please refer to Foreword for pricing information

48

DIAMOND QUILTED, "FLAT DIAMOND"

IMPERIAL GLASS COMPANY Late 1920's · Early 1930's

Colors: Pink, blue, green, crystal, black.

Pictured is a Diamond Quilted punch bowl and stand which had never been reported in green before! Isn't it exciting to find new pieces! This makes me think there is possibly a blue one out there somewhere.

A pink ice bucket has finally surfaced to accompany the blue and black; so maybe there's a green one of those around, too!

The beginning collector should know that a number of companies made a diamond quilted like pattern during this era, but Imperial's diamonds were very flat compared to most. Hence the nickname "flat diamond".

The diamond shapes are on the inside of the ebony pieces. The outside is perfectly smooth. Therefore, it is necessary to examine the interior of any black glassware you find before you can be certain it is Diamond Quilted.

Demand for blue continues to cause the price to rise in that color.

A few pieces have turned up in amber and red. Amber commands prices equal to those of blue and black; however, red demands double those. Evidentally, these colors were experimental or of an extremely limited run.

Diamond Quilted is, generally speaking, a better quality glassware than the average Depression Glass. It is less the local dime store variety and more the better department store or local jeweler's stock.

	Pink, Green	Blue, Black		Pink, Green	Blue, Black
Bowl, 4¾" Cream Soup	5.00	9.50	Mayonnaise Set: Ladle,		
Bowl, 5" Cereal	3.00	5.00	Plate, 3 Footed Dish	12.50	
Bowl, 5½", One Handle	4.50	8.00	Pitcher, 64 oz.	22.50	
Bowl, 7" Crimped Edge	5.50	9.50	Plate, 6" Sherbet	1.50	3.00
Bowl, Rolled Edge Console	15.00	17.50	Plate, 7" Salad	2.00	4.00
Cake Salver, Tall 10"			Plate, 8" Luncheon	3.00	7.50
Diameter	25.00		Punch Bowl and Stand	200.00	
Candlesticks (2 Styles) Pr.	8.50	17.50	Plate, 14" Sandwich	7.50	
Candy Jar and Cover, Ftd.	17.50	25.00	Sandwich Server,		
Compote and Cover, 11½"	32.50		Center Handle	13.50	19.50
Creamer	4.50	8.00	Saucer	1.50	3.00
Cup	3.00	4.50	Sherbet	3.50	7.50
Goblet, 1 oz. Cordial	4.50		Sugar	4.50	8.00
Goblet, 2 oz. Wine	4.50		Tumbler, 9 oz. Water	4.50	
Goblet, 3 oz. Wine	5.50		Tumbler, 12 oz. Iced Tea	5.00	
Goblet, 6" 9 oz.			Tumbler, 6 oz. Footed	4.50	
Champagne	7.00		Tumbler, 9 oz. Footed	7.50	
Ice Bucket	32.50	47.50	Tumbler, 12 oz. Footed	7.50	
			Vase, Fan, Dolphin Handles	17.50	27.50
			Whiskey, 1½ oz.	5.00	

DOGWOOD, "APPLE BLOSSOM", "WILD ROSE"
MACBETH-EVANS GLASS COMPANY 1929-1932

Colors: Pink, green, crystal, monax, cremax and yellow.

Popularity of Dogwood has increased this past year almost as dramatically as that of Georgian. Big advances of price came in pink, particularly in bowls and sherbets.

Demand has forced me to include the etched tumbler made by Macbeth-Evans which has a little band of flowers (supposedly dogwoods) etched around the top. This used to be a country cousin no one wanted in their set, preferring silk screen processed tumblers having the floral spray of dogwoods. However, due to price increase and a seeming dearth of the silk screened glasses, the more plentiful etched tumbler (as well as the perfectly plain tumblers having the shape of dogwood glasses) are suddenly very acceptable to collectors. Even that pitcher which is perfectly plain but which has the Dogwood shape (or the "S" Pattern shape) is being bought more and more by collectors to use with their sets. Though it suffices, the purist Dogwood collector would still question whether you had an undesigned Dogwood pitcher, or an undesigned "S" Pattern pitcher.

On the left of the picture are shown some cremax pieces in Dogwood. All vary in shade, cremax being a beige tinted white. Should you not be able to tell whether you have cremax or the whiter monax, put the pieces under a black light. The cremax will glow a green color while the monax will do nothing.

Green Dogwood has always been more elusive than pink, and prices mirror this fact. A few more green Dogwood pitchers and large bowls are showing up; but they are still far from plentiful. Sadly, the green bowls were frosted, drilled through and turned upside down for use as lamp shades by the company — a circumstance many collectors now ruefully view as a sad waste!

I have only seen green grill plates with the pattern around the rim; pink grill plates come both with rim pattern and all over pattern design.

An 11″ cake plate has not yet turned up in green; several in pink have been found.

Collectors of green say the 8½″ berry bowls and sherbets are very scarce; I've only seen a half dozen of the 10¼″ bowls this year.

You can see a few rare pieces of yellow Dogwood pictured on the pages of rare glass in the back of the book.

Crystal, though rather scarce, tends to be non-collectible.

Saucers in Dogwood are the same; yet cups, creamers and sugars come in both thick and thin variety in pink. Green cups seem only to be thin.

Platters are rare and very desirable.

	Pink	Green	Monax/ Cremax
*Bowl, 5½″ Cereal	7.50	9.50	12.00
Bowl, 8½″ Berry	15.00	49.50	37.50
Bowl, 10¼″ Fruit	85.00	72.50	
Cake Plate, 11″ Heavy Solid Foot	67.50		
Cake Plate, 13″ Heavy Solid Foot	37.50	35.00	
Creamer, 2½″ Thin; 3¼″ Thick	7.00	25.00 (Thin Only)	
Cup, Thin or Thick	6.00	7.50	32.50
Pitcher, 8″ 80 oz. Decorated	72.50	350.00	
Pitcher, 8″ 80 oz. (American Sweetheart Style)	425.00		
Plate, 6″ Bread and Butter	2.50	3.50	21.50
*Plate, 8″ Luncheon	3.00	4.50	
Plate. 9¼″ Dinner	9.50		
Plate, 10½″ Grill AOP or Border Design Only	6.50	9.50	
Plate, 12″ Salver	9.50		25.00
Platter, 12″ Oval (Rare)	157.50	197.50	
Saucer	3.00	3.50	15.75
Sherbet, Low Footed	12.50	25.00	
Sugar, 2½″ Thin; 3¼″ Thick	6.00	25.00 (Thin Only)	
Tumbler, 3½″, 5 oz. Decorated	57.50		
Tumbler, 4″ 10 oz. Decorated	15.00	32.50	
Tumbler, 4¾″, 11 oz. Decorated	17.50	37.50	
Tumbler, 5″, 12 oz. Decorated	22.50	42.50	
Tumbler, Etched Band	7.00		

*Yellow — $42.50

DORIC JEANNETTE GLASS COMPANY, 1935-1938

Colors: Pink, green, delphite, yellow.

The very rare, large footed Doric pitcher in green is conspicuous by its absence from this book. It was photographed for the cover; however the lab blew the print and since the pitcher and I were by then thousands of miles apart.... Oh well, I tried; and the green is just like the pink one pictured. Do please notice that equally rare yellow Doric pitcher on the cover.

That 4½", 9 oz. tumbler causing some concern is shown on the right in pink. This tumbler is patterned around the top. Green patterned around the top tumblers are next to impossible to find. Even those heavy tumblers, shown on the left in green are in short supply.

Delphite Doric is elusive except the candy and sherbets.

Coasters, cream soups, cereal bowls, salad plates, grill plates and, of course, footed pitchers are still missing from many collections.

Doric butter dishes have been slow to rise in price; yet I don't see this trend continuing for any length of time, particularly in green.

Sugar tops and candy tops are NOT interchangeable in Doric as they are in Adam and Floral patterns. Granted, they fit each other. However, the candy lid is taller and more stately looking than the sugar.

The cake plate in Doric is footed. Confusion over what is a cake plate was caused by companies sometimes making a heavy, flat plate and referring to it as a cake plate in their advertisements. However, the Doric cake plate is footed.

	Pink	Green	Delphite
Bowl, 4½" Berry	4.00	5.00	22.50
Bowl, 5" Cream Soup		47.50	
Bowl, 5½" Cereal	6.50	9.50	
Bowl, 8¼" Large Berry	8.00	9.00	67.50
Bowl, 9" Two Handled	7.50	8.50	
Bowl, 9" Oval Vegetable	8.00	9.50	
Butter Dish and Cover	47.50	52.50	
Cake Plate, 10", Three Legs	8.00	8.50	
Candy Dish and Cover, 8"	17.50	20.00	
*Candy Dish, Three Part	3.50	4.50	4.25
Coaster, 3"	6.00	9.00	
Creamer, 4"	5.50	6.50	
Cup	4.00	4.50	
Pitcher, 6", 36 oz. Flat	17.50	20.00	175.00
Pitcher, 7½", 48 oz. Footed	187.50	325.00	
(Also in Yellow at $450 00)			
Plate, 6" Sherbet	1.75	2.00	
Plate, 7" Salad	6.00	6.50	
Plate, 9" Dinner (Serrated 32.50)	5.50	6.50	
Plate, 9" Grill	6.00	6.00	
Platter, 12" Oval	7.50	10.00	
Relish Tray, 4" x 4"	3.50	4.00	
**Relish Tray, 4" x 8"	5.00	6.00	
Salt and Pepper, Pr.	21.50	24.50	
Saucer	2.00	2.25	
Sherbet, Footed	5.50	6.50	4.50
Sugar	5.00	5.50	
Sugar Cover	5.50	6.00	
Tray, 10" Handled	5.50	6.00	
Tray, 8" x 8" Serving	7.00	7.50	
Tumbler, 4½", 9 oz.	17.50	22.50	
Tumbler, 4", 11 oz. Flat	11.00	14.00	
Tumbler, 5", 12 oz.	14.50	17.00	

*Candy in metal holder — $37.50
**Trays in metal holder as shown — $27.50

Please refer to Foreword for pricing information

54

55

DORIC & PANSY JEANNETTE GLASS COMPANY, 1937-1938

Colors: Pink, crystal, green ultramarine.

Where, oh where, did all the Doric and Pansy butter dishes come from that have turned up this year? Not that the new supply hasn't quickly dried up once more, but it was fantastic to know that more were truly around to be had!

Shakers with well defined pansies are still difficult to obtain. Most collectors have given up trying to get two well struck shakers and are philosophically settling for the weaker patterned ones. It's how they were made after all!

Last time, the salad plates had made the big jump in prices. This year, it's the large 8" berry bowl leading that particular parade.

The child's set and the berry set appear to be all that was made in the pink Doric and Pansy.

Neophites should be aware that there are varying shades of the ultramarine color. Thus, unless you get all your pieces at one time, it is very unlikely that you will be able to get all of them to match. This difference is graphically illustrated by the two shades of 6 and 9 inch plates shown in the picture!

Little demand is shown for the few crystal pieces that turn up from time to time. Occasionally a sugar and creamer collector seeks said pieces in crystal.

A teal Doric & Pansy mug has turned up; so you might watch for this 7 oz. child's mug similar to the Cherry child's mug.

	Green, Teal	Pink, Crystal		Green, Teal	Pink, Crystal
Bowl, 4½" Berry	6.50	4.50	Plate, 7" Salad	20.00	
Bowl, 8" Large Berry	37.50	9.50	Plate, 9" Dinner	12.50	4.75
Bowl, 9" Handled	15.50	9.50	Salt and Pepper, Pr.	327.50	
Butter Dish and Cover	637.50		Saucer	3.50	2.25
Cup	8.00	5.00	Sugar, Open	137.50	57.50
Creamer	137.50	57.50	Tray, 10" Handled	13.50	
Plate, 6" Sherbet	8.00	6.00	Tumbler, 4½", 9 oz.	27.50	

DORIC AND PANSY
"PRETTY POLLY PARTY DISHES"

	Teal	Pink		Teal	Pink
Cup	17.25	13.50	Creamer	27.50	17.50
Saucer	4.25	3.25	Sugar	27.00	17.50
Plate	8.00	6.00	14 Piece Set	175.00	130.00

ENGLISH HOBNAIL WESTMORELAND GLASS COMPANY 1920's - 1970's

Colors: Crystal, pink; amber, turquoise, cobalt, green, blue.

Collectors search high and low for the various shades of blue in this pattern. You will see several. There are even three distinct shades of green. I am including two photographs of this pattern to show you the gamut of colors and pieces you might expect to find.

The 9¼" lamp in green and turquoise are the style most commonly seen although the latter color is not usual.

That little demitasse crystal cup is on a black amethyst saucer (pattern on the back) and is the only one of those I've seen.

Many items appear in crystal from time to time (in quantity) at the local discount houses. That is one reason I don't list crystal. I have included here the newer satin finished, ruffled comport and the bright blue footed salt dip which was made in the 1960's to make you aware that Westmoreland is still in business today! It's the older colors of this pattern that concern us as being collectible.

For those who have trouble distinguishing English Hobnail from Miss America, I offer the following observations. English Hobnail has a center motif with rays of varying distance from the center. English Hobnail hob tips are more rounded than are those of Miss America, giving the English Hobnail a smoother feel when touched. English Hobnail goblets flair out slightly at the rim and the pattern stops toward the rim and edges a plain field of glass; Miss America goblets don't flair but go straight up and they all have a set of three rings above the pattern hobs before it goes to plain glass toward the rim.

Aside from color variations to consider, notice that English Hobnail has both squared and round shaping of pieces to consider!

	Cobalt, Amber, Turquoise* Pink, Green		Cobalt, Amber, Turquoise* Pink, Green
**Ash Tray, Several Shapes	17.50	Goblet, 5 oz. Claret	12.50
Bowls, 4½", 5" Square and Round	8.00	**Goblet, 6¼", 8 oz.	13.00
Bowl, Cream Soup	10.00	Grapefruit, 6½", Flange Rim	10.00
Bowls, 6" Several Styles	9.00	Lamp, 6¼", Electric	45.00
Bowls, 8" Several Styles	15.00	**Lamp, 9¼"	75.00
**Bowls, 8" Footed and Two Handled	35.00	Lampshade, 17" Diameter (Crystal)	100.00
**Bowls, 11" and 12" Nappies	32.50	Marmalade and Cover	25.00
Bowls, Relish, Oval, 8", 9"	15.00	Pitcher, 23 oz.	75.00
Bowl, Relish, Oval, 12"	15.00	Pitcher, 39 oz.	89.50
Candlesticks, 3½", Pair	25.00	Pitcher, 60 oz.	125.00
Candlesticks, 8½", Pair	40.00	Pitcher, ½ Gal. Straight Sides	117.50
Candy Dish, ½ lb., Cone Shaped	37.50	**Plate, 5½", 6½", Sherbet	2.50
Candy Dish and Cover, Three Feet	42.50	Plate, 7¼", Pie	3.25
Celery Dish, 9"	13.50	**Plate, 8" Round or Square	5.25
Celery Dish, 12"	17.50	Plate, 10" Dinner	12.50
**Cigarette Box	19.50	Salt and Pepper, Pr., Round or Square Bases	47.50
**Cologne Bottle	20.00	Salt Dip, 2", Footed and with Place Card Holder	12.50
Creamer, Footed or Flat	12.50	Saucer	3.00
Cup	10.00	**Sherbet	9.00
Decanter, 20 oz. with Stopper	47.50	Sugar, Footed or Flat	12.50
Demitasse Cup and Saucer	22.50	Tumbler, 3¾", 5 oz. or 9 oz.	10.00
Egg Cup	21.50	Tumbler, 4", 10 oz. Iced Tea	12.50
Goblet, 1 oz. Cordial	15.00	Tumbler, 5", 12 oz. Iced Tea	15.00
Goblet, 2 oz. Wine	12.00	Tumbler, 7 oz., Footed	11.50
Goblet, 3 oz. Cocktail	12.00	Tumbler, 9 oz., Footed	12.50
		Tumbler, 12½ oz., Footed	17.50
		Whiskey, 1½ oz. and 3 oz.	15.00

*Add about 50% more for Turquoise
**Cobalt double price listed

Please refer to Foreword for pricing information

FIRE-KING DINNERWARE "PHILBE"   HOCKING GLASS COMPANY 1937-1938

Colors: Pink, green, blue, crystal.

Usually when a pattern is difficult to find or has a few known pieces, it isn't too eagerly sought by Depression Glass people. Such is definitely not the case with "Philbe". Most people would give their eye teeth to own just one piece!

Fire-King Dinnerware causes most excitement when found in blue; but pieces are extremely rare, so far, in all colors. In several years of collecting, I've only found the 6½", 15 ounce footed iced teas in blue and the pink oval vegetable bowl to be commonly found.

All three pitchers shown came from the same Ohio flea market over a seven year period. In fact, the pink one sat for three months with the $6.00 price sticker before a pitcher collector decided to buy it anyway because it was shaped like Cameo and was cheap. I understand there was a larger blue one found at the same market; but I could never trace it.

All pieces have the Cameo shape. There may be additional pieces to be found! (Cameo has so many pieces!)

At this writing, I have seen one blue cup and saucer, one green footed juice and one flat 4", 9 ounce tumbler in blue. There's bound to be more! So now that you know what it looks like, let's find it!

	All Colors
Bowl, 5½" Cereal	20.00
Bowl, 7¼" Salad	30.00
Bowl, 10" Oval Vegetable	25.00
Candy Jar, 4" Low, with Cover	95.00
Cookie Jar with Cover	100.00
Creamer, 3¼" Ftd.	22.50
Cup	42.50
Goblet, 7¼" thin, 9 oz.	97.50
Pitcher, 6" Juice, 36 oz.	250.00
Pitcher, 8½", 56 oz.	300.00
Plate, 6" Sherbet	12.50
Plate, 8" Luncheon	10.00
Plate, 10" Heavy Sandwich	15.00
Plate, 10½" Salver	15.00
Plate, 10½" Grill	12.50
Plate, 11 5/8" Salver	15.00
Platter, 12" Closed Handles	20.00
Saucer, 6" (same as sherbet)	12.50
Sugar, 3¼" Ftd.	22.50
Tumbler, 4", 9 oz. Flat Water	75.00
Tumbler, 3½" Ftd. Juice	75.00
Tumbler, 5¼" Ftd., 10 oz.	25.00
*Tumbler, 6½" Ftd., 15 oz. Iced Tea	27.50

*Blue $20.00

FIRE-KING OVEN GLASS ANCHOR HOCKING GLASS CORPORATION 1941-1950's

Colors: Pale blue, crystal.

Not begun until the war, this line of mostly kitchen ware items, proved to be one of Hocking's biggest sellers. It had a two year written guarantee for replacement if broken by oven heat. There was a caution not to use it over direct flame. Pieces listed here are from 1941, '42 and '46 catalogues. There may be additional pieces or variations of these pieces from other years. Let me know.

The most expensive pieces issued were the 2 quart covered items which retailed for $.60! Many of the smaller pieces, including the coveted 7 oz. mug, sold for $.05! Those, I believe, are what is referred to as "the good old days".

Refrigerator dishes were advertised as triple duty: bake, serve, store; and the utility bowls had four purposes: mix, bake, serve and store!

All covered bowls were sold without covers which is why you find so many which are seemingly topless. Some of the bowl covers did double duty as pie dishes, too; so here was a product which really gave you your money's worth!

The child's set pictured here in the original box sells in the $25 to $30 range, today. The set includes two pint bakers, 4 individual custards in the 6 oz. size, a rolling pin and dough tray.

Crystal sells for half the price listed for blue; but you won't find that much crystal around.

	Blue		Blue
Baker, 1 pt., rd. or sq.	1.75	Measuring Bowl, 16 oz.	4.00
Baker, 1 qt.	2.00	Nurser, 4 oz.	1.50
Baker, 1½ qt.	2.50	Nurser, 8 oz.	2.00
Baker, 2 qt.	3.00	Pie Plate, 4 3/8" Individual	1.50
Cake Pan (deep), 8¾"	5.00	Pie Plate, 5 3/8" Deep Dish	2.25
Casserole, 1 pt., Knob Handle Cover	2.50	Pie Plate, 8 3/8"	2.50
Casserole, 1 qt., Knob Handle Cover	3.00	Pie Plate, 9"	2.75
Casserole, 1½ qt., Knob Handle Cover	4.00	Pie Plate, 9 5/8"	3.50
Casserole, 2 qt., Knob Handle Cover	5.50	Pie Plate, 10 3/8" Juice Saver	6.00
Casserole, 1 qt., Pie Plate Cover	5.00	Perculator Top, 2 1/8"	1.75
Casserole, 1½ qt., Pie Plate Cover	6.00	Refrigerator Jar & Cover, 4½" 5"	2.50
Casserole, 2 qt., Pie Plate Cover	6.00	Refrigerator Jar & Cover, 5 1/8" x 9 1/8"	7.00
Casserole, 10 oz., Tab Handle Cover	4.50	Table Server, Tab Handles (Hot Plate)	4.00
Coffee Mug, 7 oz.	9.00	Utility Bowl, 6 7/8"	3.50
Cup, 8 oz. Measuring	3.00	Utility Bowl, 8 3/8"	4.50
Custard Cup, 5 oz.	1.00	Utility Bowl, 10 1/8"	5.50
Custard Cup, 6 oz., 2 Styles	1.25	Utility Pan, 10½", Rectangular	3.50
Loaf Pan, 9 1/8", Deep	3.50	Utility Pan, 8 1/8" x 12½"	5.00

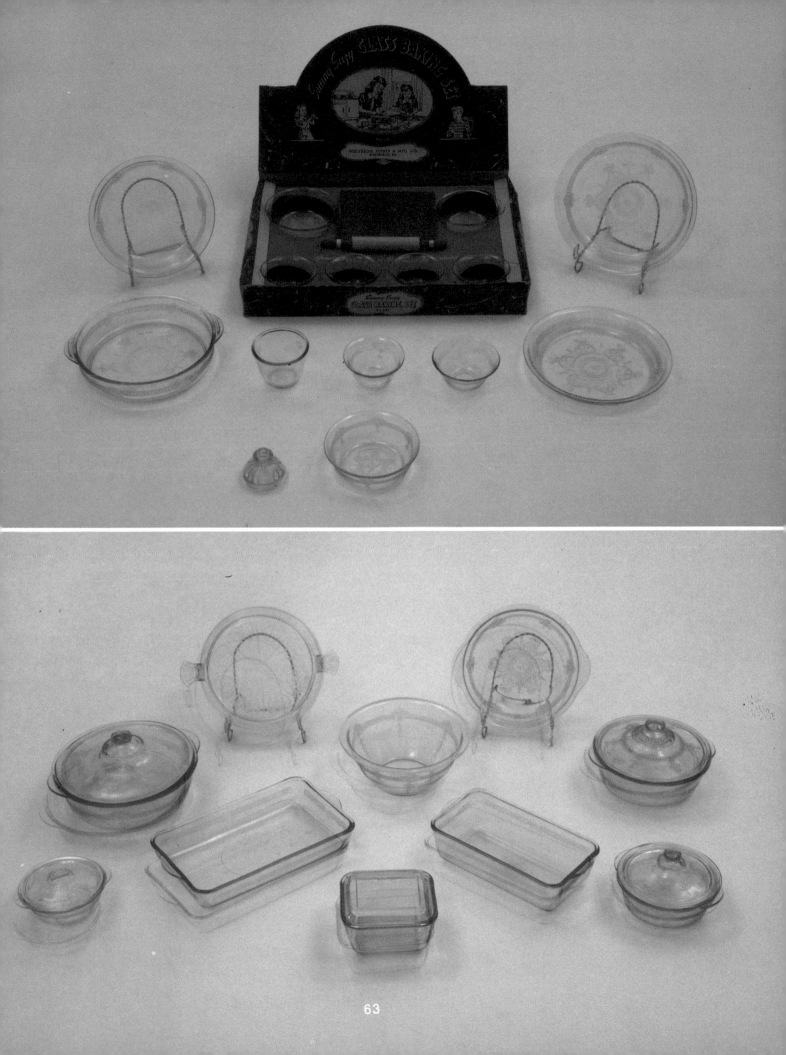

FLORAGOLD, "LOUISA" JEANNETTE GLASS COMPANY 1950's

Colors: Iridescent, pink, blue, green.

This pattern is well named; it has a floral design and it's a sprayed gold color, the color having been applied over crystal. In fact, a number of people tend to think that "Floragold" refers to this particular carnival-like color rather than being the actual name of the pattern. The pattern itself was taken from an older Carnival glass pattern known as Louisa; hence its nickname.

Unfortunately, I only found out about the Louisa Carnival pattern when I was trying to research the marvelous "find" of the rose bowl you see pictured. Alas! I goofed; for the rose bowl IS Carnival Louisa pattern rather than Floragold. They suit each other to a "T"; yet the rose bowl is much older glassware. Perhaps it was fortuitous that I hadn't done my "homework" before taking the picture. It, at least, gives a chance to view the two patterns side by side; and it provides us with what teachers love to call "a learning experience"!

Egg nog sets are available in this pattern, either having a large bowl and cups or pitcher and cups. Often these may still be packaged in their original boxes; at present, these boxes have little worth other than showing the original labeling. These sets may explain why you can find cups more readily than saucers. You will notice a significant jump in the price of saucers; and no, the saucer does not have a cup ring.

Disbelievers please notice the three sizes of tumblers shown. There are three, though there is only an ounce difference between two of them. Also notice the celery or vase which was patterned from the 15 ounce tumbler.

The candy dish which fits the sparsely found large tray with an indent is becoming scarce as well as the 5½" cereal bowl.

The price listed for shakers is for shakers with PERFECT white or brown tops. Shakers with cracked tops (caused from screwing them down too tightly) yield half the price of mint shakers. This is a case where the mint top is harder to come by than the shaker itself.

Ice blue, crystal, and red-yellow tall candy dishes and cake stands in this pattern were made in the late sixties and early seventies and have little value now. The shell pink color shown was made in the late fifties. These represent a novelty only.

	Iridescent		Iridescent
Bowl, 4½" Square	3.00	Pitcher, 64 oz.	16.50
Bowl, 5½" Cereal Round	13.50	Plate, 5¾" Sherbet	4.50
Bowl, 5½" Ruffled Fruit	3.00	Plate, 8½" Dinner	10.50
Bowl, 8½" Ruffled Fruit	2.75	Plate or Tray, 13½"	8.00
Bowl, 9½" Salad, Deep	15.00	Indent on 13½" Plate	25.00
Bowl, 12" Ruffled, Large Fruit	6.50	Platter, 11¼"	11.00
Butter Dish and Cover ¼ lb. Oblong	12.50	Salt and Pepper, Plastic Tops	25.00
Butter Dish and Cover, Round	28.50	Saucer, 5¼" (no ring)	4.50
Candlesticks, Double Branch, Pr.	19.50	Sherbet, Low Footed	6.00
Candy or Cheese Dish and Cover,		Sugar	3.00
6¾"	22.50	Sugar Lid	3.50
Candy, 5¼" Long, 4 Feet	4.00	Tumbler, 10 oz., Footed	8.00
Coaster — Ash Tray, 4"	4.00	Tumbler, 11 oz., Footed	10.00
Creamer	4.00	Tumbler, 15 oz., Footed	15.00
Cup	3.50	Vase or Celery	47.50

FLORAL, "POINSETTIA" JEANNETTE GLASS COMPANY 1931-1935

Colors: Pink, green, delphite, jadite, crystal, amber, red, yellow.

We ought to call this pattern the "surprise" pattern! In each edition of this book (three previous ones), there have been new discoveries to talk about. Rather than try to re-hash all of these in narrative for newcomers to the field, I choose rather to list past finds and direct your attention to the photographs of rare glass at the end of the book. Many of these scarce and unique items we have managed to capture on film for your viewing pleasure. The "finds" in their order of presentation since 1972 include the following: a set of DELPHITE FLORAL, a kind of opaque blue color which some call blue milk glass and which is so rare as to be virtually uncollectible; a YELLOW TWO PART RELISH dish, unique as far as presently known; an AMBER PLATE, CUP and SAUCER; GREEN JUICE PITCHERS WITH GROUND BOTTOMS, two of which are pictured here (due to the flaring of the rim, one holds 23 oz.; one, 24 oz.); FOOTED VASES similar to the rose bowl, but flared outward at the rim rather than inward (two are shown, one in green, one in crystal); a CRYSTAL LEMONADE PITCHER; the FLORAL LAMP made by notching, frosting and wiring a sherbet (one is pictured, the top, chimney and bulb being the most valuable pieces); the GREEN GRILL PLATE (shown); an EIGHT SIDED VASE with solid, round foot rather then being tri-footed, stands 6 7/8" tall, has a bottom diameter of 3½" and a top of 4 1/8" (shown on next page); a PINK RUFFLED EDGE BERRY BOWL (pictured); a PINK and GREEN FLORAL ICE TUBS (pictured on rare page in back); a PINK ruffled edge MASTER BERRY BOWL; and an OVAL VEGETABLE bowl WITH COVER in GREEN FLORAL!

At this writing a new discovery is the dresser set shown both on the cover and on the next page. It consists of a large covered jar and two smaller covered jars and they all rest on the small 9¼" tray that previously mystified people as to its use. This set netted its previous owner a tidy sum even while having the one small jar lid cracked.

Green and crystal flower frogs bearing the Floral design have also been found; they appear to fit the green and crystal flared rimmed vases.

Two new tumblers have appeared: a flat bottomed 4½", 9 oz. size which goes well with the flat bottomed pitcher; and a 3½", 3 oz. footed juice which has turned up in both green and crystal. Both are pictured at the back of the book.

A few pieces of amberina red Floral are surfacing, namely cups, saucers and plates. These, along with pieces of several other colors listed under the title were either experimental or were made at the end of a run of glass. Most of the rarer pieces of Floral which command larger prices come in green. There have been few of them found in pink. If you plan to own any of the rarer green Floral items, however, it will help if you have an oil well or two! Who knows what else will turn up in this pattern? Do keep looking; this pattern seems to have a wealth of oddities.

	Pink	Green	Delphite	Jadite
Bowl, 4" Berry (Ruffled 25.00)	4.50	5.50	21.50	
Bowl, 5½" Cream Soup		75.00		
Bowl, 7½" Salad (Ruffled 30.00)	7.00	9.00	42.50	
Bowl, 8" Covered Vegetable	17.50	20.00	37.50 (no cover)	
*Bowl, 9" Oval Vegetable	7.00	9.00		
Butter Dish and Cover	52.50	57.50		
Canister Set: Coffee, Tea, Cereal, Sugar, 5¼" Tall Set			50.00	
Candlesticks, 4" Pr.	29.50	35.00		
Candy Jar and Cover	20.00	22.50		
Creamer, Flat	5.50	6.00	50.00	
Coaster, 3¼"	5.50	6.00		
Comport, 9"	177.50	187.50		
†Cup	5.00	6.00		
Dresser Set (as shown)		900.00		
Frog for Vase		500.00		
Ice Tub, Oval 3½" High	225.00	250.00		
Lamp	67.50	67.50		
Pitcher, 5½", 23 or 24 oz.		377.50		
Pitcher, 8", 32 oz. Footed Cone	14.00	18.50		
Pitcher, 10¼", 48 oz. Lemonade	115.00	127.50		
Plate, 6" Sherbet	2.00	2.50		
Plate, 8" Salad	4.50	5.50		

	Pink	Green	Delphite	Jadite
†Plate, 9" Dinner	6.50	9.00	42.50	
Plate, 9" Grill		23.50		
Platter, 10¾" Oval	6.00	8.50	67.50	
Refrigerator Dish and Cover, 5" Square	37.50	22.50		12.50
††Relish Dish, Oval, Two Part	5.00	6.50		
Salt and Pepper, Pr. 4" Footed	25.00	27.50		
Salt and Pepper, 6" Flat	15.00	150.00		
†Saucer	4.00	5.00		
Sherbet	6.00	7.50	65.00	
Sugar	4.50	5.00	45.00 (open)	
Sugar/Candy Cover	6.00	7.50		
Tray, 6" Square, Closed Handles	5.50	6.50		
Tumbler, 4½", 9 oz. Flat		125.00		
Tumbler, 3½", 3 oz. Ftd.		75.00		
Tumbler, 4", 5 oz. Footed Juice	7.50	9.00		
Tumbler, 4¾", 7 oz. Footed Water	8.00	9.00	100.00	
Tumbler, 5¼", 9 oz. Footed Lemonade	19.50	20.00		
Vase, 3 Legged Rose Bowl		325.00		
Vase, 3 Legged Flared (Also in Crystal)		325.00		
Vase, 6 7/8" Tall (8 Sided)		325.00		

†These have now been found in amber and red.
††This has been found in yellow.
*Covered in green — 57.50

Please refer to Foreword for pricing information

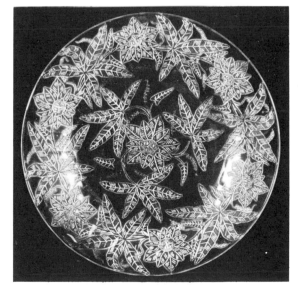

FLORAL AND DIAMOND BAND U.S. GLASS COMPANY

Colors: Pink, green, irridescent and black.

Please notice that the maker of this pattern (along with its "sister" patterns of Aunt Polly and Strawberry) has now been decided to be U.S. Glass Company rather than Jenkins Glass Company. This probably explains why some pieces of this pattern have been found in black, a characteristic color of U.S. Glass Company.

I mentioned that Floral and Diamond Band has sister patterns; this is due mainly to the fact that the three patterns share identical butter dish bottoms as well as having a certain similarity of design which is brought home to us through like finials, handle design and overall size and shape of pieces.

This pattern, though actually very attractive in a table setting, is a heavier, more cumbersome and often badly molded glassware that tends to cause would-be collectors to shy away from it initially. It is reminiscent of older glassware both in its basic solidarity and in its generously designed large creamer and sugar. One often finds large creamers and sugars in the glass of our forefathers, attesting to their sweet tooth and their less sedentary labors which allowed a delicious disregard for the caloric content of cream and sugar.

Notice the small green sugar shown. This sugar has the same pattern design, yet the flower portion is etched in the glass. Etching was seldom done in the cheaper, mass molded lines of glass simply because it took longer and required someone to do it.

I do recognize that Floral and Diamond has a definite drawback for collection by coffee lovers because of the absence of a cup and saucer.

You will find more green pieces than pink; and the greens are not always the same hue; yet this tends to be true of much of Depression Glass and shouldn't necessarily be considered a detriment — merely a characteristic of the glassware of the time.

Major price advances may be noted in the covered large sugar and the plates in green; again, the pink is scarce; but the green is more in demand.

	Green/Pink		Green/Pink
Bowl, 4½" Berry	4.00	*Pitcher, 8", 42 oz.	57.50
Bowl, 5¾" Nappy, Handled	5.50	Plate, 8" Luncheon	9.50
Bowl, 8" Large Berry	7.50	Sherbet	3.50
Butter Dish and Cover	57.50	Sugar, Small	5.00
Compote, 5½" Tall	6.50	Sugar, 5¼"	7.50
Creamer, Small	5.00	Sugar Lid	17.50
Creamer, 4¾"	9.50	Tumbler, 4" Water	7.50
		Tumbler, 5" Iced Tea	13.00

*Iridescent — $125.00

*Iridescent slightly higher and sometimes   called "Mayflower" by Carnival glass collectors.

FLORENTINE NO. 1, "OLD FLORENTINE", "POPPY NO. 1"
HAZEL ATLAS GLASS COMPANY 1932-1935

Colors: Pink, green, crystal, yellow, cobalt.

Sugar and creamer collectors should love this pattern! There are nine sets to collect: five different colored ruffled sets and four covered sets. Ruffled creamer and sugar sets are harder to find, particularly in green and yellow, though you certainly couldn't surmise this from the picture!

I am invariably asked by new collectors how to tell the difference between Florentine One and Two. It is helpful to know that Florentine One was originally advertised as Florentine Hexagonal as opposed to Florentine Round. Furthermore, only the Florentine One pieces have the serrated edges. You will find the serration in both flat and footed pieces.

(Before we go any further, I need to point out that there are eight pieces of Florentine Two down the left side of this Florentine One picture. I did this purposely during a photography session where we were switching a color picture for a black and white one previously photographed. It was the only way, at the time, to get the Florentine Two pieces included in color. Those Florentine Two pieces include the four cobalt items, the unusual large and small berry bowls in pink and the two blown flat bottomed tumblers, holding 6 oz. and measuring 3½" tall.)

I have often been asked about the possibility of Florentine One having flat bottomed tumblers like those of Florentine Two. All I can say to this is that I saw a boxed set in New England containing the footed Florentine One pitcher accompanied by six flat green tumblers having panels inside the tumblers. I had previously thought these tumblers were oddities belonging to Florentine Two; however, in light of having seen them boxed with the Florentine One pitcher, they may indeed be Florentine One. Unfortunately, there is no listing per se from the factory suggesting any flat bottomed tumbler in Florentine One.

Green is the color most collected in this pattern; crystal is the least collected though it is generally as available to the collector as any of the other colors. Crystal tends to bring about twenty-five percent less in price, save for the butter dish which is elusive and commands as big a price as does the green. However, because the crystal is less expensive, it might be a pattern worthy of consideration for new people in the field. Besides, any crystal pattern has the added advantage of not clashing with the peas!

In colors, there has been an increased demand recently for basic pieces such as cups, saucers and plates. I have noted in the past that this often portends an upward trend in overall prices. Take heed!

	Green	Yellow	Pink	Blue
Ash Tray, 5½"	12.00	22.50	22.50	
Bowl, 5" Berry	3.50	4.00	5.50	10.50
Bowl, 6" Cereal	5.00	6.50	9.00	
Bowl, 8½" Large Berry	9.00	12.00	13.50	
Bowl, 9½" Oval Vegetable & Cover	22.50	25.00	27.50	
Butter Dish and Cover	72.50	97.50	147.50	
Coaster/Ash Tray, 3¾"	9.00	9.00	18.00	
Creamer	4.00	5.00	6.50	
Creamer, Ruffled	13.50	15.00	15.00	39.50
Cup	3.00	4.00	4.50	
Pitcher, 6½", 36 oz. Footed	20.00	35.00	32.50	300.00
Pitcher, 7½", 54 oz. Flat, Ice Lip or None	30.00	80.00	80.00	
Plate, 6" Sherbet	2.00	2.00	2.50	
Plate, 8½" Salad	3.00	3.50	4.00	
Plate, 10" Dinner	6.50	7.50	9.00	
Plate, 10" Grill	4.50	5.00	6.00	
Platter, 11½" Oval	6.50	9.50	12.00	
Salt and Pepper, Footed	20.00	30.00	35.00	
Saucer	1.50	2.00	2.00	
Sherbet, 3 oz. Footed	4.00	5.50	6.00	
Sugar	3.50	5.00	7.50	
Sugar Cover	6.50	9.50	9.50	
Sugar, Ruffled	13.50	15.00	15.00	37.50
Tumbler, 3¾", 5 oz. Footed Juice	6.50	8.50	11.50	
Tumbler, 4¾", 10 oz. Footed Water	9.50	11.50	15.00	
Tumbler, 5¼", 12 oz. Footed Iced Tea	10.00	12.00	17.50	
Tumbler, 5¼", 9 oz. Lemonade (Like Floral)			42.50	

Please refer to Foreword for pricing information

FLORENTINE NO. 2, "POPPY NO. 2"

HAZEL ATLAS GLASS COMPANY 1934-1937

Colors: Pink, green, crystal, some cobalt, amber, ice blue.

Florentine Two was originally advertised as Florentine Round which helped distinguish it from the hexagonal, saw-tooth rimmed Florentine One.

This is one pattern where collecting crystal is nearly as fashionable as collecting yellow and green. In fact, the crystal butter dish may be the toughest of all this pattern's butter dishes to find.

Tops to butter dishes in Florentine One and Two are interchangeable. It's the bottom pieces which differ making the bottom the harder piece to find.

Not as many of the pattern's pieces occur in pink. For confirmation purposes I've had three persons mail me sherbets they believed to be pink Florentine Two; unfortunately, all had serrated feet rather than round ones which immediately identified them as Florentine One.

A few odd pieces in other colors exist. One lady found an ice blue pitcher in Mexico for $3.00. (See it pictured in the back). A cup, sherbet, saucer and tumbler have been found in the dark amber color; the tumbler is in this picture. A few items have surfaced in cobalt blue, such as the tumbler and the four items pictured on the left side of the Florentine One picture. (See the fourth paragraph explanation under Florentine One). The shaker pictured on the preceding page is not true cobalt. The color has been fired on over crystal, a condition which cuts the price in half. I have seen a fired on orange shaker in this pattern.

Notice those green and yellow pitchers in the background. The yellow has a handle shape more in keeping with Florentine One. However, this type pitcher was boxed from the factory with Florentine Two tumblers which strongly indicates the factory meant it to be Florentine Two.

There are TWO SIZES of the footed, cone shaped pitcher in Florentine Two. The commonly found one measures 7 1/8" tall and holds between 28-29½ ounces when filled to overflowing. The RARELY FOUND one is the shorter, chubbier version measuring 6¼" tall and holding 24-25½ ounces.

New finds in green and yellow include a flat soup with a diameter of 7½" and an odd sized small bowl measuring 5¼" in diameter.

The 5" footed tumbler holds only 9 ounces instead of the previously listed 12 ounces.

The saucer with indent fits both cup and jello dish lending itself to double service.

When encountering the hard to find candy dishes, pay particular attention to the inside rims which usually have incurred damage. Don't pay mint prices for damaged merchandise.

The pattern shot shows a Hazel Atlas Florentine No. 2 design on a Federal Madrid Shape sherbet mold!

	Crystal, Green	Pink	Yellow	Blue		Crystal, Green	Pink	Yellow	Blue
Bowl, 4½" Berry	3.50	5.00	6.50		Plate, 6¼" with Indent	7.00		12.50	
Bowl, 4¾" Cream Soup	5.00	5.50	8.50		Plate, 8½" Salad	3.00	4.50	4.50	
Bowl, 5" Cream Soup, or Ruffled					Plate, 10" Dinner	5.50	9.50	7.50	
Nut		5.00		27.50	Plate, 10¼" Grill	4.00		5.00	
Bowl, 6" Cereal	5.50	9.50	17.50		Platter, 11" Oval	6.50	8.50	8.50	
Bowl, 8" Large Berry	8.00	15.00	15.00		Platter, 11½" for Gravyboat			22.50	
Bowl, 9" Oval Vegetable and					Relish Dish, 10", 3 Part or Plain	6.00	12.00	9.50	
Cover	15.00	22.50	22.50		†Salt and Pepper, Pr.	27.50		30.00	
*Butter Dish and Cover	65.00		85.00		Saucer (Amber: 15.00)	2.00		2.50	
Candlesticks, 2¾", Pr.	23.00		27.50		Sherbet, Footed (Amber: 37.50)	5.00		6.50	
Candy Dish and Cover	57.50	85.00	77.50		Sugar	4.00		6.00	
Coaster, 3¼"	8.50	12.50	10.50		Sugar Cover	5.00		6.00	
Coaster/Ash Tray, 3¾"	9.50		12.50		Tray, Condiment for Shakers				
Coaster/Ash Tray, 5½"	15.00		22.50		Creamer and Sugar (Round)			29.50	
Comport, 3½" Ruffled	9.50	6.00	15.00	42.50	Tumbler, 3½", 5 oz. Juice	5.00	6.00	6.50	
Creamer	5.50		6.00		Tumbler, 3½", 6 oz. Blown	8.00			
Cup (Amber 35.00)	4.00		5.50		†††Tumbler, 4" 9 oz. Water	7.50	7.50	9.00	45.00
Custard Cup or Jello	17.50		22.50		Tumbler, 5" 12 oz. Iced Tea	12.50		15.00	
Gravy Boat			25.00		Tumbler, 3¼", 5 oz. Footed	7.00		7.50	
Pitcher, 6¼", 24 oz. Cone Footed			77.50		Tumbler, 4", 5 oz. Footed	7.00		8.00	
†Pitcher, 7½", 28 oz. Cone Footed	13.50		14.00		Tumbler, 4½", 9 oz. Footed	9.00		9.50	
Pitcher, 7½", 54 oz.	42.50	80.00	95.00		Tumbler, 5", 12 oz. Footed	12.00		16.00	
Pitcher, 8" 76 oz.	67.50		125.00		Vase or Parfait, 6"	15.00		20.00	
Plate, 6" Sherbet	1.50		2.25						

†Blue — $350.00
††Fired-on Orange or Blue, Pr. — 25.00
†††Amber: — 47.50

73

FLOWER GARDEN WITH BUTTERFLIES, "BUTTERFLIES AND ROSES"

U.S. GLASS COMPANY Late 1920's.

Colors: Pink, green, blue-green, canary yellow, crystal, amber, black.

Color pictures are certainly worth more to Depression Glass collectors than are black and white. After a color picture of this pattern appeared in the third edition book, several new collectors became interested in trying to net these butterflies. This, naturally, caused the prices to skyrocket and they are only just beginning to settle down into the realm of realism.

There is a blue heart-shaped candy box in North Carolina which has my wife hopeful of finding one for her collection. She'll have to find another as there is a "no sale" sign on this blue one. They have also been found in pink and canary yellow! Wow!

New items include a rectangular cigarette box and a 6" vase; but the major news is the heart-shaped candy dish.

I have discovered that some few pieces really don't have an entire butterfly resting in that mass of flowers; they may have only a partial wing or piece of an antenna. The majority do have the butterfly, however. It's just a matter of locating it.

The amber plate at the back has an indent for the compote to sit in making a cheese and cracker set.

Wall sconces, rolled edged console bowls, a rectangular cigarette box and the black vase pictured have all turned up in U.S. Glass's stand-by black color.

U.S. Glass made two size trivets with a flowered motif that some people falsely attribute to this pattern. Let me assure you that the butterfly never attempted to land on these. If you look closely, the pattern isn't even the same.

	All Colors*		All Colors*
Ash Tray, Match-Pack Holders	65.00	Cup	67.50
Bowl, Rolled Edge Console,		Plate, 8", Two Styles	9.50
2 Styles	35.00	Powder Jar, Footed	25.00
Candlesticks, 4", Pr.	25.00	Powder Jar, Flat	20.00
Candlesticks, 8", Pr.	42.50	Sandwich Server, center handle	35.00
Candy Dish and Cover, 8"	37.50	Saucer	30.00
Candy Dish, Heart Shaped	100.00	Sugar, Open	19.50
Candy Dish, Open, 6"	12.50	Tray, 5½" x 10" Oval	22.50
Cheese and Cracker Set		Tray, Rectangular, 11¾" x 7¾"	27.50
(4" Compote, 10" Plate)	32.50	Vase, 6"	50.00
Cigarette Box, 2½" x 3½"		Vase, 7" (Black)	75.00
(Black)	47.50	Vase, 10"	47.50
Cologne Bottle, 7½", Tall Footed	22.50		
Console Bowl, 10" Footed	25.00		
Creamer	19.50		

Design on Black highlighted to emphasize pattern.

*Add 25% for blue, black or canary items.

Please refer to Foreword for pricing information.

FOREST GREEN ANCHOR HOCKING GLASS COMPANY CORPORATION 1950-1957

Color: Green.

This is another non Depression Glass pattern that so many people are collecting that I have been coerced into including it. As you can tell, the predominant shape was square. Royal Ruby pieces were produced in these shapes also.

There seems little in the plain Forest Green that has turned out to be hard to get thus far save the 3-quart pitcher which goes with the abundant tumblers. Many tumblers were decorated as shown here. These decorated items tend to bring about double the price of plain ones at the moment.

	Green		Green
Ash Tray	1.25	Platter, Rectangular	6.00
Bowl, 4¾″ Dessert	1.25	Saucer	.75
Bowl, 6″ Soup	2.00	Sugar, Flat	2.50
Bowl, 7 3/8″ Salad	2.50	Tumbler, 5 oz.	1.25
Creamer, Flat	2.50	Tumbler, 10 oz.	2.00
Cup	1.50	Vase, 4″ Ivy	2.00
Plate, 6 5/8″ Salad	.75	Vase 6 3/8″	2.50
Plate, 8 3/8″ Luncheon	1.25	Vase, 9″	3.00
Pitcher, 3 qt., Rnd.	12.50		

FORTUNE HOCKING GLASS COMPANY 1937-1938

Colors: Pink, crystal.

There's good news and bad news for Fortune collectors. The good news is that there really does seem to be a pitcher to match this pattern. I've received two snapshots from readers and I've seen one at a show. The bad news is that few collectors care one way or another.

The name for this pattern which is one of those tagged on by collectors is definitely a misnomer. Few people collect it. To Hocking it was a nameless line. Perhaps the pattern ridges and spoke-like center motif suggested the wheel of fortune to someone.

At any rate, the pitcher is of interest to pitcher collectors; the candy dish is sought by a few candy dish collectors. The few hardy souls who have started collecting it as a pattern have had their hardest time locating luncheon plates.

It is probably one of the most cheaply priced patterns in Depression Glass, however; so if this is your primary concern, this is the pattern for you!

	Pink, Crstyal		Pink, Crystal
Bowl, 4″ Berry	1.00	Cup	2.00
Bowl, 4½″ Dessert	1.00	Plate, 6″ Sherbet	1.25
Bowl, 4½″ Handled	1.00	Plate, 8″ Luncheon	2.00
Bowl, 5¼″ Rolled Edge	2.00	Saucer	1.00
Bowl, 7¾″ Salad or Large Berry	3.00	Tumbler, 3½″, 5 oz. Juice	2.50
Candy Dish and Cover, Flat	9.75	Tumbler, 4″, 9 oz. Water	3.00

"FRUITS"   HAZEL ATLAS AND OTHER GLASS COMPANY 1931-1933

Colors: Pink, green, crystal.

"Fruits", a name given by collectors for obvious reasons, encompasses patterns made by several companies. You will find pieces having several types of fruits represented; you find them with perhaps only one, such as cherries or pears.

The tumbler with the cherries only which matches the pitcher is the one most in demand by collectors, particularly in green. To date, there has been no pink pitcher turn up to match the pink cherries-only tumblers. Surely there must be one!

The pink platter I received a phone call about never materialized. Is there one?

Fruit collectors have all been having difficulty finding bowls; thus, demand has greatly increased price on both; the larger 8" berry is in extremely short supply.

Iridized tumblers, usually with pears, are NOT Carnival glass and should be in the $5.00 range — not the $15 I've seen. They're frequently seen and not at all unusual or rare.

	Pink, Green			Pink, Green
Bowl, 5" Cereal	8.50	Sherbet		4.50
Bowl, 8" Berry	27.50	Tumbler, 3½", Juice		7.00
Cup	3.50	Tumbler, 4" (One Fruit)		7.50
Pitcher, 7" Flat Bottom	32.50	Tumbler, 4" (Combination		
Plate, 8" Luncheon	3.50	of Fruits)		8.00
Saucer	2.00			

HARP   JEANNETTE GLASS COMPANY 1954-1957

Colors: Crystal, crystal with gold trim.

As you can see from the dates, this glass is not Depression Glass and I've tended to ignore such patterns in the past. However, slowly but surely I'm being forced to include some of these later-made dishes since many Depression fans are collecting them.

There are no rarities in this. You will, occasionally, find a piece in the shell pink that was popularized by Jeannette in the late 1950's.

	Crystal		Crystal
Ash Tray/Coaster	2.00	Plate, 7"	2.00
Coaster	1.50	Saucer	.75
Cup	2.00	Vase, 6"	6.00
Cake Stand, 9"	7.50		

GEORGIAN, "LOVEBIRDS" FEDERAL GLASS COMPANY 1931-1936

Colors: Green, crystal.

New collectors still tend to mix up "Lovebirds" and "Parrot" even though they're not all that alike. In Georgian, or "Lovebirds", the birds alternate with a flower filled basket in the design. Too, notice the chain in the design and think of "Lovebirds" being bound by the chains of love; or remember "Lovebirds" being bound within a circle of love as this pattern is round whereas "Parrot" is squared.

It's amazing how a relatively plentiful pattern will suddenly dry up when a few hundred collectors start looking for it! This happened recently with Georgian after President Carter and the Smithsonian Institute became associated with the Georgian pattern. (See explanation on next page). Of course, some items in this pattern have never been readily available. I remarked in the 3rd edition that it had been quite a while since I'd seen a Georgian platter; the price immediately rose from $7.50 to $26.50! They are relatively scarce; but perhaps I should keep my mouth shut?

A further "run" on the pattern occurred when another author, possibly through a printing error, jumped the price on the commonly found 7½" large berry bowl when it should have been on the 6½" deep berry bowl which is rarely located. (Both are pictured. The rarely found one is in center front.) Dealers had stacks of the 7½" bowl. All of a sudden, the stacks dwindled and the price doubled. The bowl is still rather abundant; but the price now isn't indicative of the supply.

Some foolers associated with this pattern are as follows: the tumbler does not have both birds and baskets; it features only the basket; the hot plate and some dinner plates have only the border and center motif.

For an idea of how the walnut lazy susan with Georgian hot plates should look, refer to the Madrid picture.

Sugar lids for both size sugars are interchangeable; the lid is not easily found in mint condition and it is worth almost as much as the sugar bottom.

Seemingly no shakers or cream soups exist although I have had dealers who feel certain they remember having seen or having sold cream soups. As yet, I've received no confirmation of these.

	Green		Green
Bowl, 4½" Berry	3.50	†Hot Plate, 5" Center Design	22.50
Bowl, 5¾" Cereal	7.00	Plate, 6" Sherbet	2.00
Bowl, 6½" Deep	27.50	Plate, 8" Luncheon	4.50
Bowl, 7½" Large Berry	22.50	Plate, 9¼" Dinner	9.50
Bowl, 9" Oval Vegetable	29.50	Plate, 9¼" Center Design Only	8.50
Butter Dish and Cover	50.00	Platter, 11½" Closed Handled	26.50
Cold Cuts Server, 18½" Wood with		Saucer	2.00
Seven 5" Openings for 5" Coasters	275.00	Sherbet	6.00
Creamer, 3" Footed	6.00	Sugar, 3" Footed	5.00
Creamer, 4" Footed	6.50	Sugar, 4" Footed	5.50
Cup	4.50	Sugar Cover	7.50
		Tumbler, 4" 9 oz. Flat	17.50
		Tumbler, 5¼", 12 oz. Flat	27.50

†Crystal: 17.50

Please refer to Foreword for pricing information

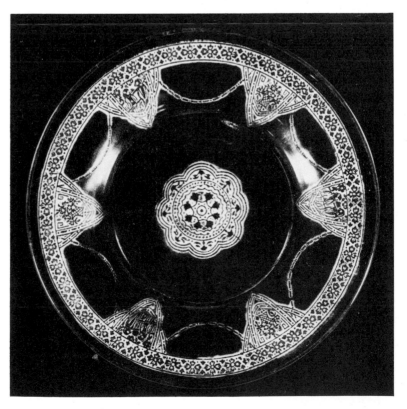

81

GEORGIAN (CON'T.)

THE PRESIDENT'S TABLE

The lovely table setting pictured here was designated as "The President's Table" by the Peach State Depression Glass Club of Marietta, Georgia. This was done in honor of President Jimmy Carter and his wife, Rosalynn on whose behalf the club donated a place setting of this pattern to the Smithsonian Institute. The butter dish from the table was presented to Mrs. Lillian Carter, the President's mother.

Not only was the place setting presented to the Smithsonian; members of the club collected and presented salad plates in most of the patterns of Depression glass. They also presented salt and pepper shakers and via advertising gave clubs throughout the country the opportunity to contribute to this communicative way of sharing and educating Americans in general about our beloved glassware. It seems fitting that this uniquely American glassware should be preserved in the Institute which is nationally associated with treasuring pieces of our heritage.

Depression Glass clubs throughout the country are beginning to gear themselves toward educating their members and the public at large about Depression Glass. This benefits everyone since the more people knowing about it tends to bring more of the glass into circulation. It's being rescued from attics and back lot buildings and placed on dining tables once again in beautiful settings such as you see here.

In the interest of helping you locate a club in your area, I will list various ones here whom I have found to be very hospitable. There are hundreds more clubs, possibly one in your city. I urge you to check them out and hopefully to become a part of them.

Colorado: Rocky Mt. Depression Glass Society, Denver — April show
Conn: Nutmeg Depression Glass Club, Southington — Late March show
    Charter Oak Depression Glass Club, Fairfield — Oct. show
Fla: Central Florida Glassaholics, Lakeland — Late Sept. show
Ga: Peach State Depression Glass Club, Marietta — 4th wk. July show
Ill: Lincolnland 20-30-40 Society, Springfield — Late April show
La: Crescent City Depression Glass Club, Metairie — 1st wk. Mar/Sept. show
Mich: Michigan Depression Glass Society, Livonia — 3rd wk. Oct. show
Mo: Gateway Depressioners, Bridgeton — 3rd wk. in Oct. show
Ohio: Cincinnati — 1st wk. Nov. show
    Western Reserve Depression Glass Club, Cleveland — last wk. Oct.
Pa: Three Rivers Depression Glass Society, Pittsburg — 1st wk. April
Wisc: 20-30-40 Society of Wisc., Milwaukee, Nov. show

The following promoters offer great shows for visitors and dealers alike:

Cameo Production	Rachel Cecil	Jim Cooper
Dixie Huckabee	Box 575	850 S. Wayne St.
12315 Dakota Pl.	Thomasville, N.C. 27360	Kenton, Ohio 43326
Yucalpa, Ca. 92399	Show: Charlotte	Show: Lima
Shows: Anaheim	2nd wk. Mar.	3rd wk. June
May & Nov. et al		

Dogwood Productions	Heavenly Productions
Trannie Davis	Joe Fitts & Pat Finnegan
4964 Bartow St. NW	582 Carpentier Way
Acworth, Ga. 30101	San Jose, Calif. 95111
Show: Marietta	Show: San Jose
1st wk. Oct. et al	Jan. June et al

HERITAGE FEDERAL GLASS COMPANY Late 1930's - 1960's

Colors: Crystal, some pink, blue, green

This is really a very dressy looking pattern on the table; I'm surprised that not more people collect it than do. It has the advantage of being in fairly good supply save for the sugars and creamers; it's economical when compared to other patterns; and it has all basic serving pieces except tumblers. This shouldn't be a drawback as any number of crystal Depression Glass tumblers would blend with the set.

Colored pieces, so far mostly berry sets, are hard to find. Blue and green are so elusive as to practically be uncollectable; yet aren't they gorgious in the picture! I have finally received a confirming photograph of a saucer in blue Heritage; so there must be a cup! It seems a lady from out west stopped at a garage sale in Georgia and bought the blue saucer for 10 cents!

Some Heritage can be found with a gold trim. It's noteworthy only as a novelty, not because it is worth any more.

	Crystal	Pink	Blue	Green
Bowl, 5″ Berry	2.00	10.00	25.00	25.00
Bowl, 8½″ Large Berry	7.50	35.00	45.00	45.00
Bowl, 10½″, Fruit	8.00			
Cup	2.50			
Creamer, Footed	6.00			
Plate, 8″ Luncheon	2.50			
Plate, 9¼″ Dinner	4.00			
Plate, 12″ Sandwich	5.00			
Saucer	1.50			
Sugar, Open Footed	5.00			

HEX OPTIC, "HONEYCOMB" JEANNETTE GLASS COMPANY 1928-1932

Colors: Pink, green.

The nickname "Honeycomb" is an obvious one in this case. Many companies made a similar hexagonal pattern. However, Jeannette's tends to be a very heavy, utilitarian type glassware.

This glassware appears to have been heavily used. Most plates are scratched and the mixing bowl you find in this pattern tends to show more scratches than design!

That ice bucket with the lip causes more discussion than anything else in the pattern. There are three current theories. One believes it to be an ice bucket. One believes that since the metal frame (see picture in 2nd edition) which fits around the piece has a bucket-like handle, it is a type of weird pitcher. Another theory is that a reamer with holes in it to let the juice flow through fitted on top; thus you needed that lip to pour out the juice. Hence, it's part of a juicer.

The 5″, 32 ounce pitcher with the sunflower motif in the bottom is placed with this line of glassware. Many mistakenly think it to be Sunflower pattern.

You will find some iridescent tumblers shaped like the ones shown. They are of much later vintage, say late fifties or early sixties.

	Pink, Green		Pink, Green
Bowl, 4¼″ Berry, Ruffled	1.50	Plate, 8″ Luncheon	2.00
Bowl, 7½″ Large Berry	3.50	Platter, 11″ Round	5.00
Bowl, Mixing	4.00	Refrigerator Dish	4.00
Butter Dish and Cover, Rectangular 1 pound Size	12.50	Salt and Pepper, Pr.	12.50
		Saucer	1.00
Creamer, 2 Style Handles	3.50	Sugar, 2 Styles of Handles	3.50
Cup, 2 Style Handles	2.00	Sherbet, 5 oz. Footed	2.50
Ice Bucket, Metal Handle	7.50	Tumbler, 3¾″, 9 oz.	2.50
Pitcher, 5″, 32 oz. Sunflower Motif in Bottom	8.50	Tumbler, 5¾″, Footed	3.50
Pitcher, 9″, 48 oz. Footed	22.50	Tumbler, 7″ Footed	4.50
Plate, 6″ Sherbet	1.25	Whiskey, 2″, 1 oz.	3.00

Please refer to Foreword for pricing information

HOBNAIL HOCKING GLASS COMPANY 1934-1936

Colors: Crystal, some pink.

Making glasses with "hobs" is rather traditional throughout the history of glass. The Depression Era companies were no different. The listing here refers to pieces Hocking made; if you have others, they were possibly made by MacBeth Evans or Imperial.

I have included in the picture the MacBeth Evans "Hobnail" pitcher and tumblers which collectors of Hocking's pink Hobnail are using with their sets as there are so few pieces of Hocking's pink. It blends very easily with their otherwise sparse sets. However, I caution that the MacBeth Evans tumblers are much more evident than the pitcher!

There are a variety of pieces in crystal although it will still take some searching to ferret them out. However, there is no 18 oz. iced tea goblet as was listed previously! The typist hit the eight key instead of the three. It should read "13 ounce goblet".

Collectors have reported to me that only luncheon sets come trimmed in red and that the red trimmed sugar and creamers are extremely difficult to locate.

	Pink	Crystal		Pink	Crystal
Bowl, 5½" Cereal		1.00	Saucer (Sherbet Plate		
Bowl, 7" Salad		1.50	in Pink)	1.25	.50
Cup	2.00	1.25	Sherbet	2.50	1.50
Creamer, Footed		1.50	Sugar, Footed		1.50
Decanter and Stopper, 32 oz.		12.50	Tumbler, 5 oz. Juice		3.00
Goblet, 10 oz. Water		4.00	Tumbler, 9 oz., 10 oz. Water		5.00
Goblet, 13 oz. Iced Tea		6.00	Tumbler, 15 oz. Iced Tea		5.00
Pitcher, 18 oz. Milk		12.00	Tumbler, 3 oz. Footed Wine		5.00
Pitcher, 67 oz.		15.00	Tumbler, 5 oz. Footed Cordial		3.75
Plate, 6" Sherbet	1.25	1.00	Whiskey, 1½ oz.		2.50
Plate, 8½" Luncheon	2.00	1.50			

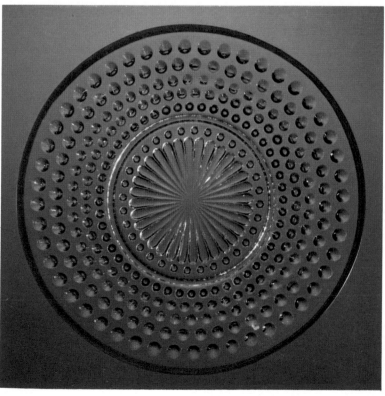

HOLIDAY, "BUTTONS AND BOWS"   JEANNETTE GLASS COMPANY 1947-1949

Colors: Pink, iridescent; some shell pink opaque and crystal.

Diminishing availability of this very late pattern has surprised many a collector. Since it was really manufactured long after the Depression, collectors expect it to be more plentiful. Butter dishes, pitchers, sugar and creamers are abundant compared to many other patterns; but the supply of other pieces is rapidly being swallowed up. The first pieces to vanish were the footed tumblers, cake plates and the 13¾" chop plate. Lately, bowls, dinner plates and even candle holders are appearing infrequently. You might expect this of an early 1930's pattern, but a late 1940's? The answer, of course, is that this is a very popular pattern. In fact, this glass was patterned after the older Daisy and Button dishes called "Buttons and Bows" by many. Since Daisy and Button had long been a popular pattern, it's success was assured. That tradition holds even today.

The smaller milk pitcher has overtaken the larger pitcher in price due to its seeming scarcity. Too, numerous collectors desire it to accompany their juice glasses.

New collectors of Holiday should be aware that there are two sizes of cups and that the cups which fit the rayed saucers are not interchangeable with the plain saucers. Check the bottom of your cup to see if it is plain or rayed and fit the saucer accordingly.

The platter, footed juice and small milk pitcher were produced in the 1950's in the iridized colors. Since a few such items have turned up in crystal, it is to be assumed that these oddities somehow managed to escape the iridizing spray at the factory. During this period of time a footed console bowl in shell pink opaque was also produced. These items are considered to be novel rather than valuable.

	Pink		Pink
Bowl, 5 1/8" Berry	4.00	Plate, 6" Sherbet	1.75
Bowl, 7¾" Soup	15.00	Plate, 9" Dinner	5.50
Bowl, 8½" Large Berry	9.50	Plate, 13¾" Chop	42.50
Bowl, 9½" Oval Vegetable	7.50	Platter, 11 3/8" Oval	6.50
Bowl, 10¾" Console	29.50	Sandwich Tray, 10½"	6.50
Butter Dish and Cover	25.00	Saucer, Two Styles	1.50
Cake Plate, 10½", 3 Legged	27.50	Sherbet	4.00
Candlesticks, 3", Pr.	32.50	Sugar	3.50
Creamer, Footed	4.50	Sugar Cover	3.50
Cup, Two Sizes	3.50	Tumbler, 4", 10 oz. Flat	10.00
Pitcher, 4¾", 16 oz. Milk	27.50	Tumbler, 4", Footed	17.50
Pitcher, 6¾", 52 oz.	22.50	Tumbler, 6", Footed	37.50

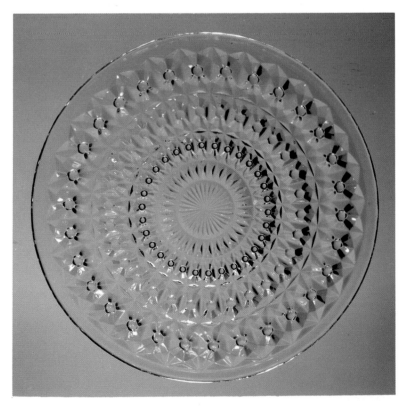

89

HOMESPUN, "FINE RIB" JEANNETTE GLASS COMPANY 1939-1940

Colors: Pink, crystal.

This pattern still can be bought and collected by beginning collectors without borrowing against the house or car. Besides, you need to have those two items free to mortgage for gasoline and food!

New collectors can readily distinguish this pattern from Hazel Atlas's "Fine Rib" by taking note of the waffle like design at the base of Homespun pieces. Most generally, Hazel Atlas's cobalt pitcher and tumblers are the culprits which generate the most confusion.

Having said that, now let me further confuse you by saying that the 96 ounce pitcher does exist in this pattern; but, alas, it does not have the waffle design in the bottom. However, this pitcher is pictured with Jeannette's own Homespun listing; therefore, we must accept it as Homespun.

Pink is presently collected more than the crystal; however, in the long run, crystal may turn out to be the better investment since therein lies the scarcely seen butter dish.

I haven't seen a child's tea pot in crystal. Have you?

That footed juice or wine (as the catalogues refer to it as both) which is 4" high and holds 5 ounces is the most often seen piece of this set. These must have been a premium item for some national product as it has turned up in all parts of the country!

	Pink/Crystal		Pink/Crystal
Bowl, 4½", Closed Handles	3.00	Platter, 13" Closed Handles	6.00
Bowl, 5" Cereal	7.00	Saucer	1.25
Bowl, 8¼" Large Berry	7.50	Sherbet, Low Flat	3.50
*Butter Dish and Cover	33.50	Sugar, Footed	3.50
Coaster/Ash Tray	3.25	Tumbler, 4", 9 oz. Water	4.50
Creamer, Footed	4.00	Tumbler, 5¼", 13 oz. Iced Tea	7.50
Cup	2.50	Tumbler, 4", 5 oz. Footed	6.50
Plate, 6" Sherbet	1.50	Tumbler, 6¼", 9 oz. Footed	6.50
Plate, 9¼" Dinner	5.50	Tumbler, 6½", 15 oz. Footed	9.50

*Crystal: 65.00

HOMESPUN'S CHILD'S TEA SET

	Pink	Crystal		Pink	Crystal
Cup	20.00	13.25	Tea Pot	20.00	
Saucer	6.25	5.00	Tea Pot Cover	27.50	
Plate	8.75	6.75	Set: 14 Pieces	187.50	
			Set: 12 Pieces		100.00

INDIANA CUSTARD, "FLOWER AND LEAF BAND" INDIANA GLASS COMPANY

Colors: Ivory or custard, early 1930's; white, 1950's.

A few years ago Indiana Custard was eagerly sought by collectors. However, difficulty in finding it caused many to give up and turn to collecting something else. As I write this, prices are increasing and it is very difficult to price pieces in a rising market. Do keep in mind what I say in the Foreword. The prices in this book are meant to be a GUIDE. They should not be construed to be the ultimate, final and only price.

The Indiana custard sherbet is the highest priced footed sherbet in Depression Glass; this is rightly so as you are viewing one of only two I've ever seen.

The biggest jump in price has been made by cups which collectors tell me have all but disappeared.

	French Ivory		French Ivory
Bowl, 4 7/8" Berry	3.25	Plate, 5¾" Bread and Butter	2.50
Bowl, 5¾" Cereal	6.50	Plate, 7½" Salad	6.00
Bowl, 7½" Flat Soup	10.00	Plate, 8 7/8" Luncheon	7.50
Bowl, 8¾" Large Berry	15.00	Plate, 9¾" Dinner	9.50
Bowl, 9½" Oval Vegetable	16.50	Platter, 11½" Oval	17.00
Butter Dish and Cover	42.50	Saucer	3.50
Cup	12.50	Sherbet	42.50
Creamer	9.00	Sugar	6.50
		Sugar Cover	8.50

Please refer to Foreword for pricing information

IRIS, "IRIS AND HERRINGBONE"

JEANNETTE GLASS COMPANY 1928-1932; 1950; 1970's
Colors: Crystal, iridescent; some pink; recently red-yellow and blue-green.

The mystery behind the short supply of saucers for the little Iris demitasse cups may have been solved by one of my readers who kindly sent me an advertisement from a woman's magazine she'd run across. In this 1947 ad it shows our little demitasse cups atop plain copper saucers being touted singly at $2.00 each or in sets of six at $11.00. It was referred to as a "demi tasse unique" which added "a delightful touch to al fresco dining".

Numerous people are writing or calling about the lamp shades and nut sets in Iris. Lamp shades made by drilling a hole in a ruffled bowl and allowing it to rest upside down over a lamp sell for about $5.00 on good days to someone who really wants one. The real shade made with a heavy glass inset in the middle and often sprayed pastel colors will sell for about $15 (on good days to someone who really wants one). As for the nut bowl sets made, again, by drilling the ruffled bowl and inserting a metal holder for nut picks and nut cracker, it took my Grannie Bear Antique shop 18 months to sell one for $17.50. I had a letter from a lady who paid $25.00 for hers. I suspect that's a good price range.

The iridized pieces done in 1969 can't be told from the earlier 1950's issue; so quit worrying about it. It just makes iridized butter dishes, pitchers, sugars and creamers easier to get.

The worrier, at present, rests in the candy bottoms and vases being sold in dish barns for $1.29 each. Mostly these appear in a red-yellow combination or a blue-green combination which is a dead give-away as being new. However, they do come in crystal. There's the rub. Upon close examination, to-day's model features a foot and candy bottom which are plain rather than rayed as were the originals. So there's no problem about telling new from old. The TOP to the candy dish has not been made new.

There are a number of pieces surfacing with a satin finish and having colored flowers painted thereon. Usually the rare 7" plate is among this lot. Perhaps that's why it's rare; they satin finished most of them! Unfortunately, collectors virtually ignore satin finish pieces. It's plain crystal Iris or nothing with them.

	Crystal	Iridescent		Crystal	Iridescent	Pink/ Green
Bowl, 4½" Berry Beaded Edge	12.50	4.00	Goblet, 5¾", 4 oz.	8.50		
Bowl, 5" Sauce, Ruffled	4.00	4.50	Goblet, 5¾", 8 oz.	10.00		
Bowl, 6" Cereal	15.00	7.50	Pitcher, 9½" Footed	15.00	17.50	
Bowl, 7½" Soup	17.50	15.00	Plate, 5½" Sherbet	2.00	2.00	
Bowl, 8" Berry	9.50	8.50	Plate, 7" Salad	20.00		
Bowl, 9" Salad	8.00	7.50	Plate, 8" Luncheon	15.00	7.50	
Bowl, 11" Fruit, Ruffled	8.50	6.00	Plate, 9" Dinner	15.50	9.50	
Bowl, 11" Fruit, Straight Edge	17.50		Plate, 11¾" Sandwich	7.50	7.50	
Butter Dish and Cover	22.50	27.50	Saucer	2.00	2.00	
Candlesticks, Pr.	13.50	17.50	Sherbet, 2½" Footed	6.50	6.00	
Candy Jar and Cover	45.00		Sherbet, 4" Footed	7.00		
Coaster	21.50		Sugar	2.50	3.50	
Creamer, Footed	3.50	4.50	Sugar Cover	3.00	3.00	
Cup	5.25	5.00	Tumbler, 4" Flat	21.50		
*Demitasse Cup	10.00	22.50	Tumbler, 6" Footed	7.50	7.50	
*Demitasse Saucer	15.00	35.00	Tumbler, 7" Footed	10.50	9.50	
Goblet, 4" Wine	9.50	10.00	Vase, 9"	9.50	11.50	27.50
Goblet, 4½" Wine	9.50					

*Ruby, Blue, Amethyst priced as Iridescent

LACE EDGE, "OPEN LACE" HOCKING GLASS COMPANY 1935-1938

Colors: Pink, some crystal.

I never cared much for Lace Edge until someone served me a fantastic meal from it with appealing decorative accoutrements placed about the table; now suddenly I'm a fan. It genuinely gives one pleasure to behold!

The candlesticks, 3 legged bowl and vase appear to be in a race to see which will first break the century price! The vase is by far the most difficult to find; so it gets my vote. In any case, the day when Lace Edge was a John Q Public's pattern has long since faded into the sunset. You now need to be among the financially elite to choose this.

Frosted or satinized pieces of the aforementioned item abound at reasonable prices; however, few people want these.

Listed for the first time is a flat juice to go with the flat water tumbler. As both of these tumblers were sold in the same ads with Lace Edge, we'll assume they belong. That reasoning has been accepted as valid for Moderntone tumblers; so why not Lace Edge?

That plate shown in the right rear is the 10½", 3 part relish omitted from the listing in the last book. Added again is the 7" vase which made the first two editions and somehow missed the third!

A footed Lace Edge tumbler was pictured in the first two editions. The rays go only halfway up the tumbler as they do in the sugar and creamer. Don't confuse Lace Edge tumblers with Coronation ones whose rays climb 2/3 to 3/4 the height of the glass.

The rays of the cup remain close to the bottom in Lace Edge; they do not climb the edge of the cup as do those of Queen Mary.

You will occasionally find green lacey edged pieces which were made by other companies such as Westmoreland or Lancaster. These are usually better quality glassware and give an angelic ring when flicked with a finger. Our Lace Edge is tone deaf however, giving off more of a "thunk". However, as I've said before, Lace Edge devotees don't collect this pattern for its tonal quality!

One word of warning: Lace Edge damages like no other due to its open spaced edges. Don't pay mint prices for damaged glass! I list prices based on MINT condition glassware only, that is glassware as near like it came from the factory as is possible, without chips, flakes, dings and chunks. I am aware that I stated all this in the Foreword of the book under pricing; but from the letters and calls I receive, I'm fast learning that some people never read the beginning pages of a book no matter how valuable the information contained therein. So, I endeavor to sneak a little of the same information under the various patterns, hoping to catch them unaware!

	*Pink		*Pink
**Bowl, 6 3/8" Cereal	5.50	Plate, 7¼" Salad	8.50
Bowl, 7¾" Salad	7.50	Plate, 8¾" Luncheon	7.50
Bowl, 9½" Plain or Ribbed	6.00	Plate, 10½" Dinner	10.00
***Bowl, 10½" 3 Legs	77.50	Plate, 10½" Grill	7.50
Butter Dish or Bon Bon		Plate, 10½" Relish 3 Part	9.50
With Cover	35.00	Plate, 13", 4 Part Solid Lace	12.50
***Candlesticks, Pr.	77.50	Platter, 13¾"	10.50
Candy Jar and Cover, Ribbed	17.50	Platter, 13¾", 5 Part	11.00
Comport, 7"	8.50	Relish Dish, 7½" Deep, 3 Part	15.00
Comport and Cover, Footed	15.50	Saucer	5.00
Cookie Jar and Cover	22.50	***Sherbet, Footed	27.50
Creamer	8.50	Sugar	8.50
Cup	7.50	Tumbler, 3½", 5 oz. Flat	4.50
Fish Bowl, 1 gal. 8 oz.		Tumbler, 4½", 9 oz., Flat	6.00
(Crystal Only)	10.50	Tumbler, 5", 10½ oz., Footed	20.00
Flower Bowl, Crystal Frog	7.50	Vase, 7"	87.50

*Satin or frosted items slightly lower in price
**Officially listed as cereal or cream soup
***Price is for absolute mint condition

95

LAKE COMO HOCKING GLASS COMPANY 1934-1937

Color: White with blue decoration.

The popularity of Lake Como has been limited to a certain extent due to few people recognizing it; however, the last year has seen more and more collectors, particularly those interested in kitchen ware, seeking this pattern.

Two different cups and saucers exist, a regular size coffee cup and the St. Denis size shown here.

Finding shakers seems extra difficult.

	White		White
Bowl, Cereal 6"	2.00	Plate, Dinner, 9¼"	3.00
Bowl, Vegetable, 9¾"	5.50	Platter, 11"	7.00
Creamer, Footed	3.50	Salt & Pepper, Pr.	12.50
Cup, Regular	2.00	Saucer	1.00
Cup, St. Denis	4.00	Saucer, St. Denis	1.25
Plate, Salad, 7¼"	1.25	Sugar, Footed	3.50

LAUREL McKEE GLASS COMPANY 1930's

Colors: French ivory, jade green, white opal and poudre blue.

Laurel had been the "Rip Van Winkle" of late in the Depression World. Even the children's items have been in little demand except for the Scotty decaled items, of course. They're always desirable.

Powder blue items are probably the most rare; but not all pieces seem to appear in blue.

Only shakers, particularly in green, have given much indication of edging upward in price.

At today's prices, this presently sleeping pattern may well be a good investment. Numerous collectors have gotten their dinner sets complete by now and are casting around for a breakfast set. Laurel would fit that bill perfectly.

Sherbets, shakers, tumblers and candlesticks are hard to get. The three legged bowl is practically impossible. That may not mean there is not a lot of this glass still around. It's possible that few people recognize it as being Depression Glass and therefore don't know its collectiblilty.

	White Opal Jade Green	French Ivory	Poudre Blue		White Opal Jade Green	French Ivory	Poudre Blue
Bowl, 5" Berry	3.00	4.00	6.50	Plate, 6" Sherbet	2.50	3.25	4.00
Bowl, 6" Cereal	4.00	5.00	7.50	Plate, 7½" Salad	2.75	5.00	7.50
Bowl, 6", Three Legs	6.00	7.50		Plate, 9 1/8" Dinner	4.50	5.00	9.00
Bowl, 9", Large Berry	8.50	11.50	15.00	Plate, 9 1/8" Grill	3.00	4.00	7.00
Bowl, 9¾" Oval				Platter, 10¾" Oval	12.50	15.00	17.50
Vegetable	12.00	15.00	21.50	Salt and Pepper	42.50	32.50	
Bowl, 10½", Three Legs	20.00	25.00	32.50	Saucer	2.00	2.50	4.00
Bowl, 11"	15.00	25.00	25.00	Sherbet	6.00	9.00	
Candlestick, 4", Pr.	15.00	20.00	25.00	Sugar, Short	6.00	7.00	12.50
Cheese Dish and Cover	37.50	47.50		Sugar, Tall	7.50	8.00	12.50
Creamer, Short	6.00	7.00		Tumbler, 4½", 9 oz. Flat		15.00	
Creamer, Tall	7.50	8.00	12.50	Tumbler, 5", 12 oz. Flat		22.50	
Cup	4.00	5.00	10.00				

CHILDREN'S LAUREL TEA SET

	Plain	Decorated Rims	Scotty Dog Decal
Creamer	17.50	27.50	32.50
Cup	12.50	17.50	22.50
Plate	7.50	12.00	15.00
Saucer	5.50	7.50	10.00
Sugar	17.50	27.50	32.50
14 Piece Set	135.00	167.50	257.50

Please refer to Foreword for pricing information

LINCOLN INN FENTON GLASS COMPANY Late 1920's

Colors: Amethyst, cobalt, black, red, green, pink, crystal, jade (opaque), green.

Lincoln Inn is a striking and well made glassware that is the first representative of the Fenton Glass Company to be included in my book. This pattern is best known for its multitude of stemware!

The salt and pepper shakers are difficult to find in any color, but they are most desirable in red. Green shakers are shown on the rare page in the back of the book.

A luncheon plate has been turned over here to better show the pattern.

Bowls are not easily found, save for the finger bowl and liner which is one of the small accessory dishes. Cereal and fruit bowls are straight of side and very shallow.

	Blue, Red	All Other Colors
Ash Tray	5.00	4.00
Bon Bon, Handled, Sq.	10.00	6.00
Bon Bon, Handled, Oval	10.00	6.00
Bowl, 5", Fruit	5.00	3.50
Bowl, 6", Cereal	7.00	4.50
Bowl, 6", Crimped	8.00	5.00
Bowl, Handled, Olive	8.00	5.00
Bowl, Finger	6.00	3.75
Bowl, 9¼", Ftd.	12.50	10.00
Bowl, 10½", Ftd.	17.50	12.50
Candy Dish, Ftd., Oval	10.00	6.50
Comport	8.00	5.00
Creamer	10.00	6.00
Cup	5.50	4.00
Goblet, Water	15.00	10.00
Goblet, Wine	12.00	8.00
Nut Dish, Ftd.	10.00	6.00
Plate, 6"	3.50	2.00
Plate, 8"	5.50	3.50
Plate, 9¼"	7.50	5.50
Plate, 12"	12.50	8.50
Salt, Pepper, Pr.	97.50	65.00
Saucer	2.50	1.75
Sherbet, 4¾"	12.00	7.00
Sugar	10.00	6.00
Tumbler, 4 oz., Flat Juice	10.00	6.00
Tumbler, 5 oz., Ftd.	11.00	7.00
Tumbler, 7 oz., Ftd.	12.00	7.50
Tumbler, 9 oz., Ftd.	12.50	8.50
Tumbler, 12 oz., Ftd.	15.00	10.00
Vase, 12", Ftd.	45.00	35.00

LORAIN, "BASKET", No. 615" INDIANA GLASS COMPANY 1929-1932

Colors: Green, yellow; some crystal.

Last year I felt the prices had gotten so high for Lorain that you had to be a true "basket case" to collect it! Yet if you bought it at last year's prices, you are now laughing all the way to the bank! It's astonishing when prices go up fifty percent in one year; but to double or even triple in price in one year is absolutely astounding!

Collectors are pouncing upon pieces of yellow Lorain as if it were the crown jewels. Yes, it is a beautiful pattern and its shapes make it rather distinctive; and yes, the topaz color of Lorain is very beautiful. It has a sort of luminescent quality to it; but how did everyone seemingly arrive at that conclusion at the same time?

Cereal bowls are as hard to find as the 8" deep berry bowl now; and the 10¼" dinner plate has skyrocketed in price as it becomes harder to get.

Mint condition saucers are more difficult to locate than are cups.

Some crystal Lorain comes to light occasionally, but not enough that I would recommend your choosing this color to collect unless you have infinite patience, devour glass ads daily and travel extensively to flea markets, glass shows, garage sales, et cetera, et ectera, et ectera (as Yul Brenner's King of Siam was fond of saying).

A few rectangular snack trays (with an off center indent for cups) have been found. These are crystal with flashed borders of red, yellow, green and blue and are selling in the $15.00 price range.

	Crystal/ Green	Yellow		Crystal/ Green	Yellow
Bowl, 6" Cereal	17.50	22.50	Plate, 9 3/8" Dinner	12.00	12.50
Bowl, 7¼" Salad	14.00	22.50	Plate, 10¼" Dinner	16.00	22.50
Bowl, 8" Deep Berry	25.00	32.50	Plate, 11½" Cake	17.50	20.00
Bowl, 9¾" Oval Vegetable	15.00	22.50	Platter, 11½"	12.00	18.50
Creamer, Footed	7.50	8.50	Relish, 8", 4 Part	8.50	11.00
Cup	4.00	5.50	Saucer	3.00	3.50
Plate, 5½" Sherbet	2.50	4.00	Sherbet, Footed	7.00	13.50
Plate, 7¾" Salad	4.50	6.00	Sugar, Footed	7.50	8.50
Plate, 8 3/8" Luncheon	5.50	7.00	Tumbler, 4¾", 9 oz. Footed	9.00	12.50

up + saucer – 9.00

Sugar – 8.50

Creamer – 8.50

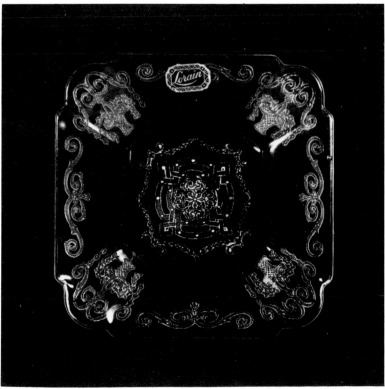

MADRID FEDERAL GLASS COMPANY 1932-1939

Colors: Green, pink, amber, crystal, "Madonna" blue.

Ostensibly as their contribution to the Bi-Centennial celebration in 1976, Federal Glass Company redesigned molds to make their "Recollection" glassware. Their "Recollection" was a new, sharper molded Madrid pattern in amber glass with a tiny little '76 date marking in the design of each piece. The amber color was a hair darker than the old. Since the glass was marked, there was little reason for collectors of amber Madrid to panic; but they had to be a little more careful that they didn't buy new butter tops on old butter bottoms. (The new butter top mold marks run through the North and South poles of the knob while the old mold marks form an equator around the middle of the butter top knob). You could get a twenty piece starter set, 4 dinners, salads, cups, saucers and soups for $19.00. The butter and cover cost you $6.00.

Federal Glass Company has now gone out of business, I understand; and many of the local discount stores offered the butter dishes at the close out price of $1.99 early in 1979. Even at this, "Recollection" was no bargain as an investment! Many major department stores in the country sold them; so there must be millions of the new pieces. Consequently, at present, I think it's a waste of money. Now by the year 2192 it might have worth; or by then we may not even use dishes to eat from---or collect. Who knows?

Old Madrid dinner plates have begun to pick up in price as collectors and dealers alike began to realize they were bargain priced since people were not all that charmed with the new ones.

The sugar lid in any color is difficult to find unmarred by chips and nicks. I've only spotted two in blue in the past year; yet surely there are more to be found.

The only other items to rise above the reproduction blues have been footed shakers in all colors.

More green footed tumblers are turning up; they used to be the rarest of the Madrid tumblers; yet there are few collectors for them and thus the prices have never soared as dramatically as on other rare items.

Walnut lazy susans have turned up in three states, Kentucky, West Virginia and Virginia. The amber gravy boat and platter has a penchant for the state of Iowa which seems to indicate regional distribution for these items. So far, only an amber gravy boat and platter have been found. I've heard rumors to the effect that a green platter has surfaced; but I can't confirm it right now.

	Crystal/ Amber	Pink	Green	Blue		Crystal/ Amber	Pink	Green	Blue
Ash Tray, 6" Square	75.00		52.50		Pitcher, 8½", 80 oz. Ice Lip	40.00		175.00	
Bowl, 4¾" Cream Soup	6.50				Plate, 6" Sherbet	2.00	2.50	2.00	4.00
Bowl, 5" Sauce	3.00	4.50	4.00	6.50	Plate, 7½" Salad	5.50	5.50	6.00	9.00
Bowl, 7" Soup	6.50		9.00	10.00	Plate, 8 7/8" Luncheon	4.00	4.50	6.00	9.00
Bowl, 8" Salad	8.00		12.50	20.00	Plate, 10½" Dinner	19.50	19.50	22.50	25.00
Bowl, 9 3/8" Large Berry	9.00				Plate, 10½" Grill	7.50		10.50	
Bowl, 9½", Deep Salad	15.00				Plate, 10¼" Relish	6.00	6.00	8.00	
Bowl, 10" Oval Vegetable	7.50	8.50	9.25	17.50	††Plate, 11¼" Cake Round	7.50	6.50	16.50	
††Bowl, 11" Low Console	7.50	7.00			Platter, 11½" Oval	6.50	7.50	9.00	13.50
Butter Dish and Cover	†47.50		52.50		Salt/Pepper, 3½", Footed	39.50		67.50	97.50
††Candlesticks, 2¼", Pr.	12.50	11.00			Salt/Pepper, 3½", Flat	27.50		49.50	
Cookie Jar and Cover	22.50	19.50			Saucer	2.00	2.00	2.50	3.50
Creamer, Footed	5.00	7.50	7.50	9.50	Sherbet, Two Styles	4.50		5.00	7.50
Cup	4.00	5.00	5.00	9.50	Sugar	3.50	4.00	6.00	8.50
Gravy Boat and Platter	500.00				Sugar Cover	17.50	35.00	20.00	47.50
Hot Dish Coaster	20.00		20.00		Tumbler, 3 7/8", 5 oz.	9.50		25.00	13.50
Hot Dish Coaster w/Indent	22.50		22.50		Tumbler, 4¼", 9 oz.	9.25	9.00	15.00	12.50
Jam Dish, 7"	12.50		11.50	20.00	Tumbler, 5½", 12 oz., 2 Styles	12.50		19.00	16.00
Jello Mold, 2 1/8" High	5.00				Tumbler, 4", 5 oz. Footed	13.50		35.00	
Pitcher, 5½", 36 oz. Juice	17.50				Tumbler, 5½", 10 oz. Footed	15.50		22.50	
Pitcher, 8", 60 oz. Square	25.00	26.50	97.50	117.50	Wooden Lazy Susan, 7 Hot				
Pitcher, 8½", 80 oz.	42.50		157.50		Dish Coasters	300.00			

†Crystal — $250.00
††(Iridescent priced slightly higher)

Please refer to Foreword for pricing information

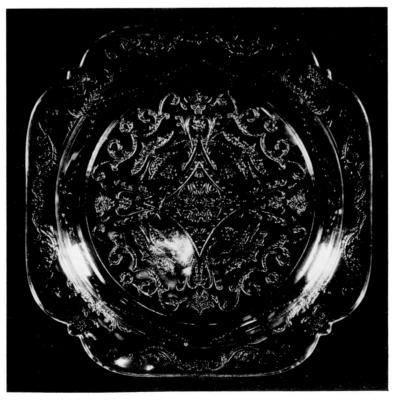

MANHATTAN, "HORIZONTAL RIBBED"

ANCHOR HOCKING GLASS COMPANY 1938-1941

Colors: Pink, crystal; some green.

At several of the bigger Depression Glass Shows I have attended recently, I was amused to see people asking dealers in vain for Manhattan. It is plentiful enough, it's just that few dealers bother to take it along to shows! This is the pattern they usually leave behind in their shops.

I have noticed an increasing desire for this glass in what I call the "now people". Manhattan is very appealing to these people. It's durable, easy to recognize, has a rather busy, yet simple and futuristic look about it the "now people" like. I find that our Grannie Bear Shop sells more Manhattan at mall shows than any other pattern; and it invariably goes to a younger couple who have never even heard of Depression Glass and have little appreciation for it once you introduce them to it. "Oh, I don't like that old stuff much; I go more for stuff they make now; and I really dig this! Whatcha call it again?"

Cups, saucers and dinner plates in crystal have jumped in price due to demand. It will still take a few years to absorb all the sugars, creamers and tumblers; yet, the reasonable price of these pieces probably makes them a decent investment.

Please notice that the tall candy with lid is priced this time. Somehow that got omitted last time and I got letters!

You will find other candle holders that appear to go with Manhattan; however, the square 4½" one shown is the only one listed by Hocking.

This wine glass goes well with the pattern; yet no information has yet surfaced to make it legitimately Manhattan.

Small pink 42 oz. pitchers are few and far between.

The lazy susan was sold with ruby, crystal and pink inserts.

	Crystal	Pink		Crystal	Pink
Ashtray, 4"	2.00	3.50	Relish Tray, 14", 5 Part	4.00	7.00
Bowl, 4½" Sauce	2.00	2.50	*Relish Tray Insert	2.00	3.00
Bowl, 5 3/8" Berry			Pitcher, 42 oz.	9.50	17.50
With Handles	2.00	2.50	Pitcher, 80 oz. Tilted	11.50	22.50
Bowl, 7½" Large Berry	3.50	4.50	Plate, 6" Sherbet	1.00	1.75
Bowl, 8" Closed Handles	3.50	4.00	Plate, 8½" Salad	2.50	3.00
Bowl, 9" Salad	4.00	8.00	Plate, 10¼" Dinner	4.00	4.50
Bowl, 9½" Fruit	4.50	9.50	Plate, 14" Sandwich	3.00	4.50
Candlesticks, 4½"			Salt/Pepper, 2", Pr.		
(Double) Pr.	6.00	12.50	(Square)	8.00	22.50
Candy Dish, 3 Legs	2.50	3.50	Saucer	1.25	2.00
Candy Dish and Cover	12.50	17.50	Sherbet	2.50	3.50
Coaster, 3½"	1.50	2.50	Sugar, Oval	2.50	4.50
Comport, 5¾"	2.50	3.50	**Tumbler, 10 oz. Footed	5.00	6.00
Creamer, Oval	2.50	4.50	Vase, 8"	4.50	7.50
Cup	2.50	3.00	Wine, 3½"	6.00	
Relish Tray, 14" 4 Part	3.00	7.50			

**Green — $5.50
*Ruby — $2.50

MAYFAIR   FEDERAL GLASS COMPANY 1934

Colors: Crystal, amber, green.

This very nice looking pattern had a limited run due to the fact that Federal discovered Hocking had already patented the "Mayfair" name. Rather than changing the name of their pattern, Federal elected to re-design their mold. What this ultimately became was the Rosemary pattern which you will find discussed later.

A further oddity will be noted, however, if you closely examine the green (handleless) sugar, the green cup, the green and amber cream soups and the amber creamer on the extreme right of the photograph. These are what are known as the "transitional" pieces. They're not quite Mayfair due to the fact that the arches on the pieces don't contain all that waffle-like effect caused by interlocking smaller arches; neither do they fit the Rosemary design, because the Rosemary pattern keeps all the arching at the tops of the pieces and leaves the bottoms perfectly plain glass. I include these transitional pieces with the regular Mayfair simply because their rarity conforms more with the prices of the lesser found Federal Mayfair than with the more common Rosemary.

Because of its limited run, Federal Mayfair is perhaps one of the rarest patterns to be collected in Depression Glass. However, the price for this pattern doesn't reflect this simply because it is so scarce that few people even try to collect it; so there is not a lot of demand for it. Scarcity and demand set prices; demand almost always overrides scarcity.

Lack of demand, therefore, has actually caused the prices in amber to drop a bit from last time.

The only item you encounter with any frequency is the green Mayfair tumbler. Were you to see ten tumblers of this pattern, nine would be in green.

	Amber	Crystal	Green
Bowl, 5" Sauce	3.50	3.00	4.50
Bowl, 5" Cream Soup	9.50	8.00	9.50
Bowl, 6" Cereal	6.50	4.00	7.50
Bowl, 10" Oval Vegetable	8.00	6.50	12.50
Creamer, Footed	6.50	5.00	7.50
Cup	4.50	3.50	5.50
Plate, 6¾" Salad	2.25	2.00	3.00
Plate, 9½" Dinner	5.50	3.50	6.50
Plate, 9½" Grill	5.00	4.00	6.00
Platter, 12" Oval	9.00	7.50	12.50
Saucer	1.75	1.25	2.00
Sugar, Footed	6.50	5.00	7.50
Tumbler, 4½", 9 oz.	8.50	6.50	9.50

MAYFAIR, "OPEN ROSE" HOCKING GLASS COMPANY 1931-1937

Colors: Ice Blue, pink; some green, yellow, crystal.   *(See Reproduction Section)*

You are viewing one of the top three patterns in Depression Glass. In fact, Mayfair may one day take precedence for collectability over Cherry Blossom and Cameo. Factors contributing to the success of Mayfair include its longevity at the factory; its traditional popularity; (nearly everybody had a piece or two of it even if they only received it as a premium for buying cookies at the store, as happened with the cookie jars); its tremendously large selection of pieces available; and the fact that, today, this is the pattern that was most often handed down from grandmother. Scores of people have bought Mayfair initially to fill in some of the hollow spots which were left when grandmother's dishes were divided between the families. Too, ice blue color in this pattern is perhaps the most beautiful blue in all of Depression Glass.

For those of you who believe that collecting yellow and green Mayfair is an impossibility, I offer the shots on the following pages as proof that it is not impossible---only expensive. I wish to thank the Earl Hines, Jr.'s and the Kelly McBrides for sharing with us the yellow and green photographed here. I could write a separate book on the difficulties encountered by all in getting these photographs; but the generosity and hospitality accorded me by these two families plus my personal satisfaction in having these pictures of this extraordinary glass to share with you make all the blown photographs, plane layovers and fog delays worth while. We all most sincerely hope you appreciate the efforts and expense! The yellow and green Mayfair is the rarest of the rare---and perfectly gorgeous!

This has been another spectacular year for discoveries in Mayfair. In pink, several odd sized goblets showed up as well as ROUND cups. In green and yellow, there are too many discoveries to discuss each separately. Of major significance were two yellow sugar lids, a yellow cookie jar and a green juice pitcher.

You may have noticed that green stemware and tumblers are showing up more than yellow; shakers and sugar lids have not yet turned up in green. We used to assume that green and yellow Mayfair were experimental pieces made by the factory; that may be true. By the number of pieces surfacing, however, I'm beginning to think that perhaps the yellow and green were made first and the colors abandoned due to roughness out of the mold or breakage. It would be nice if we could turn up some factory records to substantiate this. Evidently, much of the yellow and green was shipped into the Cincinnati, Ohio, area since nearly eighty percent of what has been found has come from there.

The very rare round cup is on the cover. Five round cups were found but they were not all alike. Two were a thin lopsided variety; three were heavier and nearly flat rimmed. Notice also the 3¾", 1 oz. liqueur; the 4", 2½ oz. wine; the 5¼", 4½ oz. claret and the unique FOOTED shaker in pink.

Take note that the 4", 2½ oz. wine has not been listed before; but it is in one of the two 1935 Hocking catalogues that I have. A reader from New England wrote me about this piece. How unusual it is needs to be determined. This wine is the same height as the cocktail, but it is shallower and holds an ounce less. While researching this piece, I also became aware that the 4¾", 11 oz. water tumbler was only listed in the one catalogue leading me to believe they enjoyed a short issue; consequently, the increased price on that particular water tumbler may have merit.

Sugar lids in pink continue to show up making them a great deal less rare than was previously thought. I mentioned I could account for about 30 in the last book; I can't be that exacting now, but I know there are more than that. However, demand for these pieces keeps the price up.

The saucer with the cup ring continues to rise sharply in price.

On the whole, the popularity of this pattern continues to grow despite the increasing prices and the reproduction of the small whiskey or shot glass. Please refer to the reproduction section at the end of the book for further enlightenment on that.

See Page 110 for Prices.

MAYFAIR, "OPEN ROSE" (Con't.)

	*Pink	Blue	Green	Yellow
Bowl, 5" Cream Soup	17.50			
Bowl, 5½" Cereal	6.00	12.50		27.50
Bowl, 7" Vegetable	11.50	25.00	65.00	75.00
Bowl, 9", 3 1/8" High, 3 Leg Console	550.00			
Bowl, 9½", Oval Vegetable	10.00	20.00	60.00	65.00
Bowl, 10" Vegetable	10.00	18.00		65.00
Bowl, 10" Same Covered	40.00	57.50		
Bowl, 11¾" Low Flat	17.50	32.50	12.00	67.50
Bowl, 12" Deep Scalloped Fruit	15.00	32.50	12.00	67.50
Butter Dish and Cover or 7" Covered Vegetable	35.00	165.00	500.00	500.00
Cake Plate, 10" Footed	12.00	30.00	49.50	
Candy Dish and Cover	25.00	85.00	350.00	300.00
Celery Dish, 9", Divided			85.00	85.00
**Celery Dish 10" or 10" Divided	10.00	19.50	75.00	75.00
Cookie Jar and Lid	19.50	77.50	325.00	325.00
Creamer, Footed	9.00	35.00	100.00	100.00
Cup	7.00	20.00	55.00	65.00
Decanter and Stopper, 32 oz	62.50			
Goblet, 3¾", 1 oz. Liqueur	225.00		225.00	
Goblet, 4" Cocktail, 3½ oz.	33.50		200.00	
Goblet, 4½" Wine, 3 oz.	37.50		200.00	
Goblet, Claret, 5¼", 4½ oz.	250.00		250.00	
Goblet, 5¾" Water, 9 oz.	22.50		200.00	
Goblet, 7¼" Thin, 9 oz.	67.50	60.00		
Pitcher, 6", 37 oz.	20.00	45.00	300.00	300.00
Pitcher, 8", 60 oz.	25.00	57.50	250.00	250.00
Pitcher 8½", 80 oz.	27.50	87.50	275.00	275.00
Plate, 6" (Often substituted as saucer)	4.00	6.50	20.00	20.00
Plate, 6½" Round Sherbet	6.50			
Plate, 6½" Round, Off Center Indent	15.00	15.00	55.00	
Plate, 8½" Luncheon	8.50	13.50	45.00	45.00
Plate, 9½" Dinner	20.00	24.50	60.00	60.00
Plate, 9½" Grill	12.50	17.50	45.00	45.00
Plate, 12" Cake W/Handles	10.00	20.00	12.00	
Platter, 12" Oval, Open Handles	10.00	18.00	90.00	90.00
Platter, 12½" Oval Closed Handles, 8" Wide				145.00
Relish, 8 3/8", 4 part or Non-Partitioned	9.50	25.00	90.00	90.00
Salt and Pepper, Pr. Flat.	29.50	110.00		375.00
Salt and Pepper, Pr., Footed	1,500.00			
Sandwich Server/Center Handle	12.00	28.50	12.00	75.00
Saucer (Cup Ring)	11.75			
Saucer (See 6" Plate)				
Sherbet, 2¼" Flat	50.00	45.00		
Sherbet, 3" Footed	9.00			
Sherbet, 4¾" Footed	35.00	32.50	115.00	115.00
Sugar, Footed	11.50	35.00	80.00	80.00
Sugar Lid	477.50			500.00
Tumbler, 3½", 5 oz. Juice	15.00	42.50		
Tumbler, 4¼", 9 oz. Water	13.50	35.00		
Tumbler, 4¾", 11 oz. Water	35.00	55.00	125.00	
Tumbler, 5¼", 13½ oz. Iced Tea	20.00	45.00		
Tumbler, 3¼", 3 oz. Footed Juice	40.00	37.50		
Tumbler, 5¼", 10 oz. Footed	14.50	36.50		115.00
Tumbler, 6½", 15 oz. Ftd. Iced Tea	19.00	43.50	145.00	
Vase, (Sweet Pea)	57.50	35.00	87.50	
Whiskey, 2¼", 1½ oz.	50.00			

*Frosted or satin finish items slightly lower
**Divided Pink Celery — $35.00

Please refer to Foreword for pricing information

111

MISS AMERICA, (DIAMOND PATTERN)   HOCKING GLASS COMPANY 1935-1937

Colors: Crystal, pink; some green, ice blue and red.   *(See Reproduction Section)*

Would you believe Diamond Pattern was the first name used by Hocking to refer to Miss America? Wonder why they changed it? I'll bet it had some promotional reason tied up with the Miss America Pageant or a certain "Miss America" taking the country by a storm. Does any one have an old magazine ad featuring said girl and glass together?

Please be certain to refer to the reproduction section in the back of this book before you spend a pocket full of money on a butter dish. I don't care how old the previous owner was, these reproductions are strewn from one end of the country to the other now. I've told you definite ways to tell the old from the new; so learn it all before you spend your hard earned cash for the butter dish.

Except for the butter dish and shakers, nothing else is being reproduced in this pattern at this time. Watch the trade papers, a few of which are listed at the back of the book. They keep you informed about reproductions.

The price of harder to get items in pink continues to soar. There is greater demand than supply in pink for pitchers, candy dishes, divided relish dishes, goblets and tumblers.

Sorry, due to a printing error in the last book under green, five pieces were priced below the salad plate which do not exist. As I got no letters about this, it seems to have confused only my plagiarist. I do apologize, however, for not catching it.

A few items in red or ice blue surface from time to time; but these settle more into the area of conversation pieces rather than having tremendous value.

I am removing the tid-bit servers from the listings of glass except in American Sweetheart where there is one with an expensive fifteen inch plate. Yes, they do exist and once were a delight to find. However, so many of the ones you see today have been recently "Manufactured" in that people are drilling through regular plates and taking newly made or old hardware and "putting them together" and making a tidy profit. Therefore, I'm just leaving them out. If you want one for your collection and don't care whether it was made in the 1930's or put together last week, then by all means get it. Personally, I'd as soon do without unless I personally knew that all of it was genuinely old.

If the piece you found isn't in the listing below, check Enlglish Hobnail pattern. Miss America tends to have uniform raying of pieces and three rings around the top of its stemware. English Hobnail has hexagonally patterned rays and clear glass edges rising directly from the diamond-like pattern.

The unusual Jadite plate used in the pattern shot has been turned upside down in order to show the pattern more clearly.

	Crystal	Pink	Green	Red		Crystal	Pink	Green	Red
Bowl, 4½" Berry			7.00		***Plate, 5¾" Sherbet	2.50	3.50	5.00	
*Bowl, 6¼" Berry	4.00	7.00	9.00		Plate, 6¾"			6.00	
Bowl, 8" Curved in at top	22.50	35.00		225.00	Plate, 8½" Salad	3.50	8.50	8.00	52.50
Bowl, 8¾" Straight Deep Fruit	20.00	32.50			****Plate, 10¼" Dinner	7.50	13.00		
Bowl, 10" Oval Vegetable	9.00	11.00			Plate, 10¼" Grill	6.50	9.50		
**Butter Dish and Cover	187.50	350.00			Platter, 12¼" Oval	9.50	11.00		
Cake Plate, 12" Footed	12.50	19.50			Relish, 8¾", 4 Part	6.00	9.00		
Candy Jar and Cover, 11½"	40.00	67.50			Relish, 11¾" Round Divided	10.00	37.50		
Celery Dish, 10½" Oblong	6.50	8.50			Salt and Pepper, Pr.	20.00	30.00	257.50	
Coaster, 5¾"	12.00	17.50			Saucer	2.50	3.00		
Comport, 5"	7.50	10.50			Sherbet	5.50	9.00		
Creamer, Footed	5.50	8.00		100.00	Sugar	4.50	7.50		100.00
Cup	6.00	11.00	8.00		Tumbler, 4", 5 oz. Juice	12.50	27.50		
Goblet, 3¾", 3 oz. Wine	13.50	35.00		125.00	Tumbler, 4½", 10 oz. Water	10.00	16.50	13.50	
Goblet, 4¾", 5 oz. Juice	15.00	37.50		125.00	Tumbler, 6¾", 14 oz. Iced Tea	18.00	33.00		
Goblet, 5½", 10 oz. Water	12.50	24.50		125.00					
Pitcher, 8", 65 oz.	45.50	70.00							
Pitcher, 8½", 65 oz. W/Ice Lip	47.50	75.00							

*Also has appeared in Cobalt Blue — $100.00
**Absolute mint price
***Also in Ice Blue — $30.00
****Also in Ice Blue — $52.50

Please refer to Foreword for pricing information

113

MODERNTONE, "WEDDING BAND"   HAZEL ATLAS GLASS COMPANY 1934-1942

Colors: Amethyst, cobalt blue; some crystal, pink and platonite fired-on colors.

Since some people collect anything cobalt blue, we have gathered a few outsiders into the ranks of Depression Glass via Moderntone. Prices continue to climb for the blue despite there being a fairly good supply of most pieces. Now, having said that, I'll add that the small berry bowl and the soup bowl are practically relics of the past. That's one of those items dealers and collectors alike remember "back when . . .".

The tumbler shown and listed here was made by Hazel Atlas in blue, pink, green and crystal. It was not officially listed as belonging to Moderntone; but it was sold in the blue color the same time as Moderntone; therefore, many collectors include it with their set. (This same reasoning applies to the Lace Edge flat tumblers).

Demand for and availability of the blue causes it to rise in price; scarcity of the amethyst is the contributing factor to its cost.

There are a few platonite collectors beginning to show up.

The butter dish has a ledge for the metal lid to rest around; yet many cereal bowls are being sold as butter bottoms.

The metal lids were not made at Hazel Atlas; yet since they crop up so frequently on Moderntone, it is to be assumed they were supplied by another manufacturer.

Cheese dishes should have the wooden cutting board.

A few pink and crystal items pop up from time to time; these have little significance except the ash tray.

Platonite, which occurs in Newport and Ovide patterns also, refers to a special heat resistant ware that was marketed by Hazel Atlas. It normally came with fired-on colors.

	Cobalt	Amethyst	Platonite Fired On Colors		Cobalt	Amethyst	Platonite Fired On Colors
*Ash Tray, 7¾", Match Holder in Center	67.50			Plate, 5¾" Sherbet	2.00	2.50	.75
				Plate, 6¾" Salad	2.50	3.00	1.00
Bowl, 4¾" Cream Soup	6.00	7.50		Plate, 7¾" Luncheon	4.00	3.50	1.25
Bowl, 5" Berry	7.50	5.00	.75	Plate, 8 7/8" Dinner	6.00	5.50	2.00
Bowl, 5" Cream Soup,				Plate, 10½" Sandwich	9.50	8.00	2.50
Ruffled	6.50	8.00	1.25	Platter, 11" Oval	8.50	8.00	2.00
Bowl, 6½" Cereal	8.00	9.00	1.00	Platter, 12" Oval	9.00	8.50	2.00
Bowl, 7½" Soup	15.00	12.50	1.50	Salt and Pepper, Pr.	17.50	20.00	8.00
Bowl, 8¾" Large Berry	12.00	12.50	3.00	Saucer	1.50	1.50	.75
Butter Dish With				Sherbet	4.00	3.50	2.00
Metal Cover	50.00			Sugar	4.50	4.50	2.00
Cheese Dish, 7" With				Sugar Lid in Metal	15.00		
Metal Lid	62.50			Tumbler, 5 oz.			2.50
Creamer	4.50	4.50	2.00	Tumbler, 9 oz.	6.00		3.00
Cup	3.50	3.00	1.00	Tumbler, 12 oz.			3.00
Cup (Handle-less)				Whiskey, 1½ oz.	3.50		3.00
or Custard	5.50	5.50					

*Pink — $87.50

MOONDROPS NEW MARTINSVILLE 1932-1940

Colors: Amber, pink, green, cobalt, ice blue, red, amethyst, crystal, dark green, light green, jadite, smoke, black.

Once again I am going to list all colors of Moondrops at the same price level. Do keep in mind, however, that the red or cobalt color will bring a little more due to demand; and that crystal will bring slightly less than the prices listed due to lack of demand. A twenty percent price differential above and below the base prices is a good range from which to work.

Avid collectors of this pattern are still searching for the covered pieces, pitchers and the "rocket" and "winged" styled pieces. "Bee hive" items are not quite as popular.

Rarely do you find a pattern in Depression Glass where the flat pieces are the most difficult to find. However, Moondrops is one such pattern. Even if you don't collect it, don't pass a flat piece by as you will find a market for it either via direct sales or trading.

The tray to the miniature creamer and sugar is a difficult find. Notice its dividing ridge and shape in the pattern shot.

	All Colors		All Colors
Ash Tray	8.50	Goblet, 6¼", Water, 9 oz.	13.50
Bowl, 5¼", Berry	4.00	Mug, 5 1/8", 12 oz.	12.50
Bowl, 6¾", Soup	8.00	Perfume Bottle, "rocket"	25.00
Bowl, 7½", Pickle	9.50	Pitcher, Small, 6 7/8", 22 oz.	77.50
Bowl, 8 3/8", Footed, Concave Top	12.00	Pitcher, Medium, 8 1/8", 32 oz.	115.00
Bowl, 8½", Three Footed, Divided Relish	9.50	Pitcher, Large With Lip, 8", 50 oz.	125.00
Bowl, 9½", Three Legged, Ruffled	12.50	Pitcher, Large, No Lip, 8 1/8", 53 oz.	125.00
Bowl, 9¾", Oval Vegetable	17.50	Plate, 5 7/8", Bread and Butter	2.50
Bowl, 9¾", Covered Casserole	45.00	Plate, 6 1/8", Sherbet	2.50
Bowl, 9¾", Two Handled, Oval	25.00	Plate, 6" Round, Off-Center Indent for Sherbet	4.00
Bowl, 11½", Celery, Boat Shaped	17.50	Plate, 7 1/8", Salad	4.00
Bowl, 12", Three Footed, Round Console	22.50	Plate, 8½" Luncheon	4.50
Bowl, 13", Console with "wings"	27.50	Plate, 9½" Dinner	8.50
Butter Dish and Cover	325.00	Plate, 15" Round Sandwich	13.00
Candles, 2", Ruffled, Pr.	17.50	Plate, 15", Two Handled Sandwich	22.50
Candles, 4½", Sherbet Style, Pr.	15.00	Platter, 12" Oval	12.50
Candlesticks, 5", "wings", Pr.	32.50	Saucer	3.00
Candlesticks, 5¼", Triple Light, Pr.	35.00	Sherbet, 2 5/8"	6.50
Candlesticks, 8½", Metal Stem, Pr.	20.00	Sherbet, 4½"	8.50
Candy Dish, 8", Ruffled	12.50	Sugar, 2¾"	8.00
Cocktail Shaker, with or without handle, metal top	15.00	Sugar, 4"	6.50
Comport, 4"	7.50	Tumbler, 2¾", Shot, 2 oz.	6.50
Comport, 11½"	16.50	Tumbler, 2¾", Handled Shot, 2 oz.	7.50
Creamer, 2¾", Miniature	8.00	Tumbler, 3¼", Footed Juice, 3 oz.	7.50
Creamer, 3¾", Regular	5.50	Tumbler, 3 5/8", 5 oz.	6.00
Cup	6.50	Tumbler, 4 3/8", 7 oz.	7.50
Decanter, Small, 7¾"	27.50	Tumbler, 4 3/8", 8 oz.	8.50
Decanter, Medium, 8½"	32.50	Tumbler, 4 7/8", Handled, 9 oz.	9.50
Decanter, Large, 11¼"	37.50	Tumbler, 4 7/8", 9 oz.	10.00
Decanter, "rocket", 10¼"	47.50	Tumbler, 5 1/8", 12 oz.	10.50
Goblet, 2 7/8", ¾ oz. Liquer	12.50	Tray, 7½", For Miniature Sugar/Creamer	15.00
Goblet, 4", 4 oz. Wine	9.50	Vase, 7¾", Flat, Ruffled Top	32.50
Goblet, 4¼", "rocket" Wine	17.50	Vase, 9¼", "rocket" style	52.50
Goblet, 4¾", 5 oz.	8.00		
Goblet, 5 1/8", Metal Stem Wine	8.50		
Goblet, 5½", Metal Stem Wine	8.50		

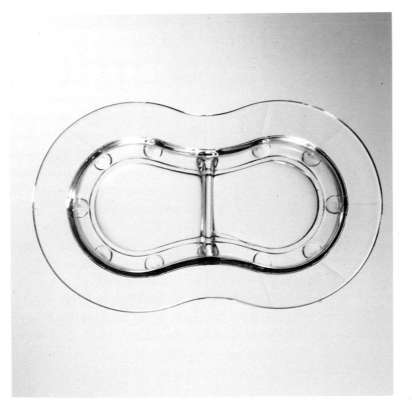

117

MOONSTONE ANCHOR HOCKING GLASS CORPORATION 1941-1946

Color: Crystal with opalescent hobnails.

When setting Moonstone on display at a mall show, I'll invariably get someone walking by who will exclaim, "Why, I've got some of those! I went to housekeeping with that!" Strictly speaking, this is not truly a Depression Era pattern. It was marketed during World War II in luncheon sets as gift items; consequently, many a war bride does have pieces of it stuck back in the cabinet, saved mostly in memory of the person who gave the piece to her. However, once she sees it displayed, you often hear, "Well, I'm going to get that back out!"

Moonstone is becoming more collectible as time advances. The 5½" berry bowl and the 6½" crimped, handled bowl have already become difficult to find.

I get numerous letters about pitchers, shakers and stemmed water goblets which are adamantly pronounced to be Moonstone. The more pointed hobs of these will usually identify them as having been made by Fenton Glass Company rather than Anchor Hocking. The listing below tells explicitly what items in Moonstone pattern were made by Anchor Hocking. If you wish to purchase the similar Fenton pitcher and tumblers to go with your set, I see no harm in doing so. Few people will know the difference!

Notice the raised rays and the one set of hobs appearing in the bottom of the flat pieces of Moonstone. Observe also the unusual **green** bowl used as a pattern shot!

This is one of the less expensive patterns to collect so far; and it dresses any table well!

	Opalescent Hobnail		Opalescent Hobnail
Bowl, 5½" Berry	6.00	Cup	4.50
Bowl, 5½" Crimped Dessert	4.50	Goblet, 10 oz.	9.50
Bowl, 6½" Crimped, Handled	5.50	Heart Bonbon, One Handle	6.00
Bowl, 7¾" Flat	6.50	Plate, 6¼" Sherbet	2.00
Bowl, 7¾" Divided Relish	6.50	Plate, 8" Luncheon	5.00
Bowl, 9½" Crimped	8.50	Plate, 10" Sandwich	8.00
Bowl, Cloverleaf	7.50	Puff Box and Cover, 4¾", Round	11.50
Candleholder, Pr.	12.50	Saucer (Same as Sherbet Plate)	2.00
Candy Jar and Cover, 6"	12.50	Sherbet, Footed	5.00
Cigarette Jar and Cover	11.50	Sugar, Footed	5.00
Creamer	5.00	Vase, 5½" Bud	8.50

119

MT. PLEASANT, "DOUBLE SHIELD"   L.B. SMITH COMPANY 1920's-1934

Colors: Black amethyst, cobalt blue, green, pink.

Little demand due to the limited availability of Mt. Pleasant relegates this to a lesser collected pattern. However, due to its colors of black, amethyst and cobalt, Mt. Pleasant will always have collectors be they Depression Glass collectors or not!

A few more sets of the gold trimmed saucers with the crystal cups have turned up in the original boxes.

I've included as a pattern shot a black sandwich server with a Dogwood design silk screened onto it. I have a large two handled bowl with the same processing.

Mt. Pleasant was an expensive glass when it was first made as compared with the cheaper "free when you purchase . . ." glassware that is commonly thought of as the average Depression Glass. It gets it's "double shield" name from the little "shield" design appearing to mirror itself top to bottom.

	Pink, Ebony, Green	Black Amethyst, Amethyst, Cobalt		Pink, Ebony, Green	Black Amethyst, Amethyst, Cobalt
Bon Bon, Rolled Up Handles	9.00	13.50	Cup	4.00	6.50
Bowl, 3 Footed, Rolled-In Edges, As Rose Bowl	11.00	15.50	Plate, 8" Scalloped or Square	6.00	8.50
Bowl, 8" Scalloped, Two Handles	10.00	14.50	Plate, 8" Solid Handles	7.00	12.00
Bowl, 8" Two Handled Square	9.50	15.00	Plate, 10½" Cake with Solid Handles	12.50	17.50
Candlesticks, Single Stem, Pr.	12.00	15.00	Salt and Pepper Shakers (Two Styles)	14.00	20.00
Candlesticks, Double Stem, Pr.	15.00	22.50	Saucer, Square or Scalloped	2.00	2.50
Creamer (Waffle-like Crystal)	4.50		Sherbet, Scalloped Edges	5.00	9.00
Creamer (Scalloped Edges)	7.00	10.50	Sugar (Waffle-like Crystal)	5.00	
Cup (Waffle-like Crystal)	3.00		Sugar (Scalloped Edges)	7.00	9.50

NEW CENTURY, and incorrectly, "LYDIA RAY"
HAZEL ATLAS GLASS COMPANY 1930-1935

Colors: Green; some crystal, pink, amethyst and cobalt.

The picture of New Century shows what I found to be a novel idea; at least it was worth the $.50 price tag at the garage sale! Someone had taken a sherbet, added the sugar lid and made a powder jar. It's just as I found it, marble decoration and all!

An amethyst cup and saucer as well as a cobalt cup have been found in recent months; there must be other pieces around! Until now, only pitcher and tumbler sets have been found in these colors; that cobalt color assures this pattern of collection by someone!

Covered casseroles, decanters with stoppers, wines and cream soups are difficult to locate. I suspect that if six more people decided to collect this that even the pieces which are considered to be more plentiful would soon be in short supply! You just don't see much of this around.

Elsewhere Ovide pattern has been incorrectly called New Century. You might wish to look at Ovide now to see how completely different it is from New Century.

	Green, Crystal	Pink, Cobalt, Amethyst		Green, Crystal	Pink, Cobalt, Amethyst
Ash Tray/Coaster, 5 3/8"	19.00		Plate, 7 1/8" Breakfast	3.50	
Bowl, 4½" Berry	3.50		Plate, 8½" Salad	4.00	
Bowl, 4¾" Cream Soup	7.50		Plate, 10" Dinner	6.00	
Bowl, 8" Large Berry	9.00		Plate, 10" Grill	5.00	
Bowl, 9" Covered Casserole	32.50		Platter, 11" Oval	7.50	
Butter Dish and Cover	42.50		Salt and Pepper, Pr.	21.50	
Cup	3.50	8.50	Saucer	2.00	3.50
Creamer	5.00		Sherbet, 3"	4.50	
Decanter and Stopper	27.50		Sugar	4.50	
Goblet, 2½ oz. Wine	7.50		Sugar Cover	5.50	
Goblet, 3¼ oz. Cocktail	8.50		Tumbler, 3½", 5 oz.	6.00	5.50
Pitcher, 7¾", 60 oz., with or without Ice Lip	19.50	20.00	Tumbler, 4 1/8", 9 oz.	7.50	6.00
Pitcher, 8", 80 oz. with or without Ice Lip	21.00	27.50	Tumbler, 5", 10 oz.	8.00	7.50
Plate, 6" Sherbet	1.75		Tumbler, 5¼", 12 oz.	10.50	8.25
			Tumbler, 4", 5 oz. Footed	7.50	
			Tumbler, 4 7/8, 9 oz. Footed	9.00	
			Whiskey, 2½", 1½ oz.	5.50	

NEWPORT, "HAIRPIN" HAZEL ATLAS GLASS COMPANY 1936-1940

Colors: Cobalt blue, amethyst, pink, "Platonite" white and fired-on colors.

As with New Century and some other minor patterns, collectors are drawn to Newport because of its cobalt and amethyst colors. There are numerous people out there who collect just amethyst colored glass (or cobalt) irregardless of the fact that it belongs to some specific category of glassware such as Depression Glass.

Amethyst Newport is pretty; yet because there is not all that much of this color around, it isn't a dynamic seller; right, Bobby? It is rather rare; but its basic scarcity has precluded many people being interested in it. It's hard to have a proclivity for something you seldom see.

Due to some previous listing misplacement by another author, Newport shakers are known to some as "Petalware" shakers. If you collect Petalware and don't mind the slightly different design, these shakers will fill in nicely. You should know there are two shades of the white, however. One is a kind of opalescent white while the other is similar to heavy milk glass.

There are few collectors of the "fired-on" Platonite colors though there are some. One gentleman told me he figured he'd buy it while it was still reasonable.

	*Cobalt	Amethyst		*Cobalt	Amethyst
Bowl, 4¼" Berry	2.50	3.50	Plate, 11½" Sandwich	11.50	13.50
Bowl, 4¾" Cream Soup	6.00	7.50	Platter, 11¾" Oval	12.50	14.50
Bowl, 5¼" Cereal	3.00	4.50	Salt and Pepper	20.00	22.50
Bowl, 8¼" Large Berry	9.50	12.50	Saucer	2.00	2.50
Cup	3.00	4.00	Sherbet	4.00	5.50
Creamer	4.50	5.00	Sugar	4.50	5.00
Plate, 6" Sherbet	2.00	2.50	Tumbler, 4½", 9 oz.	8.00	10.00
Plate, 8½" Luncheon	4.00	5.00			

*WHITE 60% of Cobalt price.

NORMANDIE, "BOUQUET AND LATTICE"

FEDERAL GLASS COMPANY 1933-1940

Colors: Iridescent, amber, pink, crystal.

Scarce items of Normandie in pink now include sugar lids, dinner plates, shakers, pitchers and tumblers. After that, what's left to collect? The pink has all been the rage recently; consequently, a lot of the supply has been grabbed up. Whether this is a permanent condition or not remains to be seen. Hopefully, more can be ferreted out of storage in barn lofts and chicken houses and some other unusual out buildings where I've heard stories of its location.

You won't believe this, but iridescent salad plates are hard to find. I know; you didn't think anything could be hard to find in that color which we believed to have few fans. There must have been enough to collect most of the salad plates!

Pink Normandie is rather rare and desirable; thus, prices have risen. Amber, at present, isn't as "saleable". The iridized is most often seen and the only trouble with it comes from convincing some uninformed person that they don't have rare "Carnival" plates or cups and saucers!

	Amber	Pink	Iridescent		Amber	Pink	Irdescent
Bowl, 5" Berry	3.00	4.00	4.00	Platter, 11¾"	6.00	8.50	7.50
*Bowl, 6½" Cereal	5.00	6.50	6.00	Salt and Pepper, Pr.	25.00	35.00	
Bowl, 8½" Large Berry	6.50	8.00	7.50	Saucer	1.75	2.00	1.75
Bowl, 10" Oval Veg.	8.00	15.00	10.00	Sherbet	4.00	5.00	4.50
Creamer, Footed	4.00	4.50	5.00	Sugar	3.00	3.00	4.00
Cup	3.50	3.50	4.00	Sugar Lid	45.00	75.00	
Pitcher, 8", 80 oz.	37.50	57.50		Tumbler, 4", 5 oz.			
Plate, 6" Sherbet	1.75	2.00	2.00	Juice	9.50	20.00	
Plate, 8" Salad	4.00	5.50	7.50	Tumbler, 4¼", 9 oz.			
Plate, 9¼" Luncheon	3.50	4.50	5.00	Water	8.50	15.00	
Plate, 11" Dinner	7.50	22.50	7.50	Tumbler, 5", 12 oz.			
Plate, 11" Grill	5.00	6.50	5.50	Iced Tea	12.50	19.50	

*Mistaken by many as butter bottom.

Please refer to Foreword for pricing information

123

NO. 610, "PYRAMID" INDIANA GLASS COMPANY 1926-1932

Colors: Green, pink, yellow; some crystal; black, 1974-75 by Tiara.

As was the custom with Indiana Glass Company, they issued this line of glassware a number. Collectors have given it its name, "Pyramid".

Though Pyramid has a limited supply as do some others, it has not been written off as "uncollectible" by Depression Glass addicts. On the contrary, in spite of its infrequent appearance, die hard collectors have pushed up the price on all pieces of all colors! The most eagerly sought color, however, is yellow with the ice tub and lid representing the creme de la creme of pieces. In this case it is the lid that is the toughest to obtain.

After searching in vain for over two years for the oval vegetable and pickle bowls to photograph for the third edition book, I found four oval vegetable bowls and one pickle dish within a three week period---just after I'd photographed the book! It's uncanny; but there's always one pattern that "does this to me" every book! They're included now though!

Oval bowls have pointed edges; pickle bowl edges are rounded. I have since located a yellow pickle dish. Maybe next time!

The crystal pitcher was located the weekend before photographing the last book. Since that time (nearly three years), I have only seen one other. Thus, the crystal pitcher is a real find for the pitcher collectors! Any other pieces in crystal would probably be so rare as to be virtually uncollectible---unless the phenomenon remarked on in the second paragraph would encompass crystal as well.

	Crystal/Pink	Green	Yellow
Bowl, 4¾" Berry	4.50	5.50	12.50
Bowl, 8½" Master Berry	8.50	9.50	22.50
Bowl, 9½" Oval	17.50	17.50	27.50
Bowl, 9½" Pickle	17.50	17.50	27.50
Creamer	7.50	8.50	12.50
Ice Tub	22.50	27.50	37.50
Ice Tub and Lid	52.50	57.50	97.50
Pitcher	92.50	75.00	157.50
Relish Tray, 4 Part, Handled	17.50	17.50	27.50
Sugar	7.50	8.50	12.50
Tray for Creamer and Sugar	9.50	10.00	15.00
Tumbler, 8 ounce, Footed	10.50	12.00	17.50
Tumbler, 11 ounce, Footed	16.50	17.50	27.50

NO. 612, "HORSESHOE" INDIANA GLASS COMPANY 1930-1933

Colors: Green, yellow; some pink, crystal.

Collectors whose horses wore decidedly fancier shoes than those our Kentucky horses use dubbed this pattern "Horseshoe" for Indiana.

A few collectors have expressed their doubt about the existence of the three sizes of bowls in Number 612, those being the 7½", the 8½" and the 9½". I assure you we had all three sizes at the photography session. However, we wound up eliminating one due to its messing up the symmetry the photographer felt he had at last achieved in at least one of the picture set ups! Thus, it's missing due to our yielding to the demands of art!

Only creamers and sugars have turned up thus far in crystal.

Please notice the platter which does not carry the overall design in the base. This variance occurs also in the dinner plate if you ever get the opportunity to make this observation! Dinner plates are tough!

Few new collectors are tackling "Horseshoe". Price has become an obstacle and, as is the case with many of Indiana's patterns, the distribution was limited to a small section of the country.

As things stand now, the Number 612 butter dish remains one of the most expensive in Depression Glass.

The 9 ounce flat tumbler is more plentiful than the 12 ounce flat one. Footed iced teas have all but disappeared from the market.

	Green	Yellow		Green	Yellow
Bowl, 4½" Berry	8.50	10.00	Plate, 8 3/8" Salad	4.00	4.50
Bowl, 6½" Cereal	8.50	10.00	Plate, 9 3/8" Luncheon	6.00	6.00
Bowl, 7½" Salad	9.50	12.50	Plate, 10 3/8" Dinner	12.00	12.50
Bowl, 8½" Vegetable	14.50	17.50	Plate, 10 3/8" Grill	15.00	15.00
Bowl, 9½" Large Berry	17.50	22.50	Plate, 11" Sandwich	6.50	7.50
Bowl, 10½" Oval Vegetable	11.50	13.50	Platter, 10¾" Oval	12.00	12.50
Butter Dish and Cover	437.50		Relish, 3 Part, Footed	8.50	9.50
Candy in Metal Holder			Saucer	2.75	3.25
Motif on Lid —			Sherbet	8.00	9.50
Also, Pink— ($97.50)	92.50		Sugar, Open	7.00	7.00
Creamer, Footed	7.50	7.50	Tumbler, 4¼", 9 oz.	45.00	
Cup	4.50	5.50	Tumbler, 4¾", 12 oz.	67.50	
Pitcher, 8½, 64 oz.	167.50	172.50	Tumbler, 9 oz., Footed	9.00	10.00
Plate, 6" Sherbet	2.00	2.50	Tumbler, 12 oz., Footed	45.00	57.50

127

NO. 616, "VERNON"   INDIANA GLASS COMPANY 1930-1932

Colors: Green, crystal, yellow.

Number 616 is another Indiana pattern of limited distribution; to further hinder its collectibility, there are so few pieces to the set! The picture shows you everything you can possibly have to date.

Green "Vernon" seems more difficult to locate than other colors.

You can find the crystal trimmed with a platinum band which adds a bit of elegance and looks smashing with the good silver!

For a while we were using crystal tumblers daily; however, after that second one broke, I couldn't stand the strain and retired them to the china cabinet! My wife believes things you like should be used and enjoyed rather than having them rusticate. I got to really liking Arby's cartoon glasses!

	Green	Crystal	Yellow
Creamer, Footed	19.50	10.00	17.50
Cup	13.00	5.50	11.00
Plate, 8" Luncheon	6.50	5.50	7.25
Plate, 11" Sandwich	15.00	12.50	17.50
Saucer	4.50	2.75	4.25
Sugar, Footed	19.50	10.00	17.50
Tumbler, 5", Footed	23.00	11.00	20.00

NO. 618, "PINEAPPLE & FLORAL"   INDIANA GLASS COMPANY 1932-1937

Colors: Crystal, amber; some fired-on red, green; Late 60's: avocado.

The light green plate shown here in Pineapple & Floral remains the only piece to surface in this color though the man I bought it from assured me at the time that he had other pieces of green. So, where is it?

I'm constantly confronted with an avocado colored comport in Pineapple & Floral. This is new glass made in the late 60's and early 1970's. Avocado color was really big then, remember? You could even get stoves and refrigerators in it. These comports sold at our local dish barn at about $.79. You could also get the crystal and sundry other colors. Thus, comports in amber and fired-on red are all you can be certain of having achieved any degree of aging.

I mistakenly left out of my listing the 4¾" berry bowl last time. It's about the diameter of the cream soup and it is relatively hard to find. I notice it was listed in my first edition and somehow got overlooked thereafter.

Cereal bowls, oval vegetable bowls and cream soups have gotten scarce. Other pieces are easily located.

You will find extreme mold roughness (in this case, excess glass around the seams of the pieces), to be a general characteristic of Pineapple & Floral.

	Crystal	Amber/Red		Crystal	Amber/Red
Ash Tray, 4½"	12.50	15.00	Plate, 11½" Sandwich	8.00	9.50
Bowl, 4¾" Berry	15.00	10.00	Platter, 11" Closed Handles	6.50	6.50
Bowl, 6" Cereal	13.50	10.00	Platter, Relish, 11½",		
Bowl, 7" Salad	4.50	5.50	Divided	12.00	6.50
Bowl, 10" Oval Vegetable	12.00	10.50	Saucer	2.00	2.00
Comport, Diamond Shaped	1.00	4.00	Sherbet, Footed	7.50	7.00
Creamer,			Sugar, Diamond Shaped	5.50	6.50
Diamond Shaped	5.50	6.50	Tumbler, 4", 9 oz.	12.00	14.50
Cream Soup	12.00	12.50	Tumbler, 4¼", 10½" oz.	14.00	17.50
Cup	4.50	5.50	Tumbler, 4½", 12 oz.	17.50	16.00
Plate, 6" Sherbet	2.00	3.00	Vase, Cone Shaped	17.50	
Plate, 8 3/8" Salad	3.50	4.00	Vase Holder (17.50)		
*Plate, 9 3/8" Dinner	6.50	7.00			

*Green — $17.50

Please refer to Foreword for pricing information

129

OLD CAFE HOCKING GLASS COMPANY 1936-1938; 1940

Colors: Pink, crystal, ruby red.

As in Coronation pattern, Hocking made a red Old Cafe cup during their Royal Ruby promotion of the 1940's and sold it on a crystal saucer. I've been asked why. I don't know. Possibly some ad man at the time thought it a brilliant idea; maybe they had a lot of crystal saucers left over in the warehouse. Maybe it was symbolic of the bloody upheavals of war as opposed to the wavering clarity of peace. Who knows why?

Most people who purchase Old Cafe get occasional pieces to blend with other patterns or they buy the Royal Ruby.

I would advise anyone stumbling onto a dinner plate to get it. They aren't easily found and you should be able to sell it easily to a collector or perhaps trade it for something you want yourself.

I have seen the 7¼" vase in Ruby turned upside down and made into a lamp.

	Crystal, Pink	Royal Ruby		Crystal, Pink	Royal Ruby
Bowl, 3¾" Berry	1.50	3.50	Plate, 6" Sherbet	1.00	
Bowl, 5", One or Two Handles	2.50		Plate, 10" Dinner	7.50	
Bowl, 5½" Cereal	3.50	7.50	Saucer	1.50	
Bowl, 9", Closed Handles	4.00	9.00	Sherbet, Low Footed	2.50	
Candy Dish, 8" Low	5.00	9.00	Tumbler, 3" Juice	3.00	
Cup	2.50	4.00	Tumbler, 4" Water	4.00	
Lamp	7.50	13.00	Vase, 7¼"	7.50	12.00
Olive Dish, 6" Oblong	3.00				

OLD ENGLISH, "THREADING" INDIANA GLASS COMPANY

Colors: Green, amber; some pink, crystal.

New pieces continue to turn up in Old English. My listing consists of what I have seen as I have not been able to find an official listing from the company.

I have pictured a 5¾", 8 oz. goblet, a flat candy dish and a 4" flat berry bowl which I had not listed previously.

There are a few really avid collectors of Old English, particularly in green.

The flat candy is most often found in a metal holder.

The pitcher lid can readily be distinguished from the candy top because the pitcher lid has a pouring notch in it. Hold the lid as you pour, however. The top justs rests up there; it doesn't snap in or on like plastic lids we're used to using!

	Pink, Green Amber		Pink, Green Amber
Bowl, 4" Flat	8.50	Plate, Indent for Compote	11.50
Bowl, 9" Footed Fruit	15.00	Sandwich Server, Center Handle	17.50
Bowl, 9½" Flat	17.50	Sherbet	9.50
Candlesticks, 4", Pr.	17.50	Sugar	7.50
Candy Dish & Cover, Flat	25.00	Sugar Cover	12.50
Candy Jar with Lid	27.50	Tumbler, 4½" Footed	8.50
Compote, 3½" Tall, 7" Across	9.00	Tumbler, 5½" Footed	15.00
Creamer	8.50	Vase, 5 3/8", Fan Type, 7"	
Fruit Stand, 11" Footed	17.50	Across	17.50
Goblet, 5¾", 8 oz.	12.50	Vase, 12" Ftd.	22.50
Pitcher and Cover	67.50		

Please refer to Foreword for pricing information

OVIDE, incorrectly dubbed "New Century"
HAZEL ATLAS GLASS COMPANY 1930-1935
Colors: Green, black, white, platonite trimmed with fired-on colors.

This pretty "Art Deco" decorated Ovide continues to cause the only stir in this pattern. Though infrequently found, when found it continues to come from the area of Northeastern Ohio and Western Pennsylvania. I need to warn you Depression Glass collectors that there are "Art Deco" enthusiasts around now who will beat you to this if they can.

White was made during the 1933 - 1935 period at Hazel Atlas and given the name "Platonite". This glass was supposed to have special heat resistant properties and it cost more than other glassware at the time. They usually fired-on colorful trims such as those rings around the restaurant grade plate at the back or the all-over color of that yellow cup and saucer.

The shapes of Ovide are like those of Cloverleaf and Ribbon patterns. A black Ovide candy dish was found. Refer to the Cloverleaf pattern to see how the candy is shaped.

	Green	Black/ Decorated White		Green	Black/ Decorated White
Bowl, 4¾" Berry		6.50	Plate, 6" Sherbet	1.00	2.50
Bowl, 5½" Cereal		6.50	Plate, 8" Luncheon	1.50	5.00
Bowl, 8" Large Berry		13.50	Plate, 9" Dinner		7.00
Candy Dish and Cover	12.50	20.00	Platter, 11"		9.00
Cocktail, Fruit, Footed	1.50	5.50	Salt and Pepper, Pr.	7.50	17.50
Creamer	2.50	7.50	Saucer	1.25	3.00
Cup	1.50	5.00	Sherbet	1.50	6.50
			Sugar, Open	2.50	7.50

OYSTER AND PEARL ANCHOR HOCKING GLASS CORPORATION 1938-1940
Colors: Pink, crystal, ruby red, white with fired on pink or green.

Candle holders and the monsterous 13½" sandwich plate in pink are the items most generally seen in Oyster & Pearl. Since setting my size 10½ foot right in the middle of the big plate when unpacking from a photography session, I have an instinctive aversion to this sandwich server.

The pink coloring fired-on over white was called "Dusty Rose"; the fired-on green coloring was christened "Springtime Green". Both colors tend to look nicer in this picture than en realite.

Red pieces made for the 1940 Royal Ruby promotion at Anchor Hocking sell better than any other color.

The pattern consists only of occasional pieces; give it consideration when you need a Depression Glass serving piece to blend with your sets.

The large fruit bowls make excellent salad serving bowls for buffets.

	Crystal, Pink	Royal Ruby	White With Fired On Green Or Pink
Bowl, 5¼" Round or Handled	2.25	7.50	4.50
Bowl, 5¼" Heart Shaped, One Handled	3.50		4.50
Bowl, 6½" Deep, Handled	6.50	9.50	
Bowl, 10½" Fruit, Deep	6.50	17.50	9.00
Candleholder, 3½", Pr.	7.50	22.50	10.00
Plate, 13½" Sandwich	5.50	17.50	
Relish Dish, 10¼" Oblong	4.00		6.00

Please refer to Foreword for pricing information

"PARROT", SYLVAN FEDERAL GLASS COMPANY 1931-1932

Colors: Green, amber; some crystal.

I've no more fantastic quantities to report such as the 37 Parrot pitchers found in the basement of an old hardware store. What made that story better was the fact that until then, no parrot pitchers were known. However, I've a tantalizing rumor to report. Supposedly a cookie jar has been located in Texas. I can't confirm it; but that's the "hearsay".

(While I'm down around the border here, let me pass on some other scuttlebutt. Several interesting pieces have crossed the border from Mexico of late, namely square footed Princess tumblers, a footed Princess pitcher, a Floral rose bowl and as mentioned, the ice blue Florentine pitcher was found here. So, if you're traveling there, it might behoove you to look up their flea markets and junk shops).

More collectors are starting to turn to the amber Parrot causing the limited supply of serving pieces to be noticeable.

Green butter dishes have been equal to the demand; but hot plates and shakers have gone into hiding.

When shopping for Parrot, carefully check out the pointed ridges on the cups, sherbets, etc. These tend to be flaked and chipped. The prices listed are for MINT items, not those with even the tiniest of chips.

There are round, thin, green luncheon plates around with parrots and flowers in the design which were made by Indiana Glass Company. These do not belong to Federal's forested Sylvan!

Amber grill plates are squared; green Parrot grill plates are round.

	Green	Amber		Green	Amber
Bowl, 5" Berry	6.50	6.00	Plate, 10¼" Square	12.50	12.50
Bowl, 7" Soup	13.00	12.50	Platter, 11¼" Oblong	12.50	32.50
Bowl, 8" Large Berry	32.50	35.00	Salt and Pepper, Pr.	122.50	
Bowl, 10" Oval Vegetable	15.00	17.50	Saucer	5.50	5.50
Butter Dish and Cover	152.50	425.00	Sherbet, Footed, Cone	9.50	8.50
Creamer, Footed	10.00	12.50	Sherbet, 4¼" High	47.50	
Cup	10.00	9.50	Sugar	8.50	10.00
Hot Plate, 5"	137.50		Sugar Cover	32.50	47.50
Pitcher, 8½", 80 oz.	350.00		Tumbler, 4¼", 10 oz.	40.00	47.50
Plate, 5¾" Sherbet	5.50	5.50	Tumbler, 5½", 12 oz.	42.50	47.50
Plate, 7½" Salad	8.50		Tumbler, 5¾" Footed,		
Plate, 9" Dinner	12.50	13.50	Heavy	42.50	47.50
Plate, 10½" Grill, Round	8.50		Tumbler, 5½", 10 oz.		
Plate, 10½" Grill, Square		8.50	Thin (Madrid Mold)		67.50

135

PATRICIAN, "SPOKE" FEDERAL GLASS COMPANY 1933-1937

Colors: Pink, green, amber, yellow.

A patrician was a Roman nobleman. I feel we do this particular pattern a disservice when we refer to it simply as "Spoke" because whoever designed Patrician for Federal went to a great deal of trouble to embody some Roman characteristics. His museum preserved chariot wheel is echoed in the center motif. Notice the various types of borders used on the edges of the pattern. Borders were very significant to Romans as well as certain drapings of the toga. A purple border around an elaborately draped toga set a nobleman apart from persons of lower rank. Indeed, borders were so significant that the Roman incorporated them into his buildings and tombs, intricate and beautiful borders such as those seen here on the Patrician pattern. Since the designer so artfully and thoughtfully constructed this design, we owe him at least the tiny homage of recognizing his work by its name, Patrician!

Would you believe that those once plentiful amber dinner plates are finally being absorbed into collections? It's taken quite a few years to exhaust the supply of these as they evidently were well promoted! My Dad even recognized Patrician as being the set of dishes he'd won as a child for selling the most newspapers!

Pitchers, tumblers, cookie jars and bowls in amber have fallen far short of the demand. The flat iced tea has doubled in price and the footed tumbler almost has! Even luncheon and salad plates have gone up!

The applied handled pitcher, illustrated here by the crystal pitcher, is harder to find than the pitcher with the molded handle. However, you should be so lucky as to get to pick and choose! Patrician pitchers of any type are not all that common.

Mint condition sugar tops and cookie bottoms are difficult in all colors. Also, the heavy lidded butter top seems to have contributed to making butter bottoms a lot harder to find. Evidently there were a lot of lid "lifters and bangers" during the Depression, too! ("Lifters and bangers" is a dealer term used to describe the less than careful lookers at a Depression Glass show---the uneducated who don't know that a chip or flake lowers the price of a dish!)

	Amber, Crystal	Pink	Green		Amber, Crystal	Pink	Green
Bowl, 4¾", Cream Soup	5.50	11.50	12.50	Plate, 9" Luncheon	4.50	4.50	4.50
Bowl, 5" Berry	4.50	9.50	5.00	Plate, 10½" Dinner	3.50	13.50	15.00
Bowl, 6" Cereal	9.00	12.50	9.50	Plate, 10½" Grill	5.00	8.50	8.50
Bowl, 8½" Large Berry	10.00	12.50	12.00	Platter, 11½" Oval	6.50	9.50	9.50
Bowl, 12" Oval Vegetable	9.50	10.00	8.50	Salt and Pepper, Pr.	27.50	57.50	37.50
Butter Dish and Cover	47.50	195.00	75.00	Saucer	3.00	3.50	3.50
Cookie Jar and Cover	39.50		155.00	Sherbet	4.50	8.50	8.50
Creamer, Footed	5.00	7.50	5.00	Sugar	3.00	5.50	4.00
Cup	3.50	4.50	4.00	Sugar Cover	17.50	37.50	32.50
Pitcher, 8", 75 oz.	52.50	87.50	67.50	Tumbler, 4", 5 oz.	10.50	15.00	15.50
Pitcher, 8¼", 75 oz.	52.50	97.50	79.50	Tumbler, 4½", 9 oz.	10.50	12.50	12.50
Plate, 6" Sherbet	2.00	2.50	2.50	Tumbler, 5½", 14 oz.	20.00	42.50	25.00
Plate, 7½" Salad	5.50	12.50	7.50	Tumbler, 5¼", 8 oz.			
				Footed	22.50		32.50

137

"PEACOCK AND WILD ROSE", LINE #300 PADEN CITY 1930's

Colors: Pink, green.

Paden City didn't "name" its glass or their etchings but gave them numbers! This nickname was obviously inspired by what is pictured on the etching. I, frankly, had never paid much attention to etched Depression Glass until I stumbled onto a big selection of this at one time. It's better quality ware; there doesn't appear to be a lot of it; and you'll find prices ranging from the ridiculous to the sublime.

Since there were no complete catalogue listings for this pattern, I am including what I have found and their particular measurements. You will probably find additional items.

	Pink/Green		Pink/Green
Bowl, 8½", Flat	12.50	Candlesticks, 5" Across, Pr.	15.00
Bowl, 8½", Oval Fruit, Ftd.	15.00	Candy Dish and Cover, 7"	22.50
Bowl, 8¾", Ftd.	12.50	Comport, 6¼"	11.50
Bowl, 9¼", Ftd.	14.00	Creamer, 4½", Ftd.	9.50
Bowl, 9¼", Center Handled	15.00	Ice Bucket, 6"	25.00
Bowl, 10½", Fruit	17.50	Ice Tub, 4¾"	22.50
Bowl, 10½", Ftd.	17.50	Mayonnaise, 3 Pc.	20.00
Bowl, 10½", Center Handled	15.00	Plate, 10½"	12.50
Bowl, 11", Console	14.00	Relish, 3 Part	10.00
Bowl, 14", Console	22.50	Sugar, 4¼", Ftd.	9.50
Cake Plate	14.00	Vase, 10"	30.00

"PEACOCK REVERSE", LINE 412 PADEN CITY

Colors: Cobalt blue, red.

This lovely glassware turns up in antique shows where Depression Glass per se is frowned upon. Our latest finds were red candlesticks with the reverse peacock design etched on either side of the base. Unfortunately, they were coupled with a foreign made red bowl and labeled "Cambridge".

These pieces have what is commonly called the "crow's foot" background. Actually, the "crow's foot" is what made this line #412. The reverse peacock etching would have been given a number by the company.

	Red/Blue		Red/Blue
Bowl, 4 7/8", Squared	12.50	Plate, 5¾", Sherbet	10.00
Bowl, 8¾", Square	25.00	Sherbet, 4 5/8" Tall, 3 3/8" Diameter	15.00
Bowl, 8¾", Square with Handles	27.50	Sherbet, 4 7/8" Tall, 3 5/8" Diameter	15.00
Candlesticks, Sq. Base, 5¾", Pr.	50.00	Sugar, 2 ¾", Flat	20.00
Creamer, 2¾", Flat	20.00	Tumbler, 4", 10 oz., Flat	25.00

PETALWARE   MACBETH EVANS GLASS COMPANY 1930-1940

Colors: Pink, crystal, monax, cremax, cobalt and fired-on yellow, blue, green & red.

Over the years, Petalware has begun to "grow on me" as they say. I find I'm not the only one as I've run into more and more devotees of Petalware in the last couple of years. This is particularly true of the Petalware with some design on it such as birds, flowers or fruit. I was particularly elated to find the Florence Cherry plate! There are seven other fruits to be found in this set.

The plate in the left rear is hand painted and artist initialed "EZ". It wasn't done at the factory; but someone's handiwork appealed to me, so I bought it.

I think the Pennsylvania Dutch design with the blue birds is unusual. Notice the two varities of luncheon plate designs having blue birds.

Red Flower decorated items occur in sherbets, cereal bowls and berry bowls also; but they aren't as plentiful as the basic luncheon set. To my thinking, the red bordering added the perfect touch.

All pieces shown here are the Monax; the beige or clam colored Petalware called Cremax by Macbeth Evans was shown in the 3rd edition. Cremax can also be found with fruit decorations or having colored bands circling it.

There are quite a few pieces having entirely fired-on colors of blue, red, green and yellow; so far, these have little appeal to collectors. One such blue cup was shown in the 3rd edition. The true, transparent blue is quite rare but not plentiful enough to be in great demand except by people who specialize in collecting Depression Glass rarities.

There is a cobalt blue mustard jar with an attached plate and having a metal top that is commonly found.

You will also find chandeliers and lamps having petalware shades.

There are no salt and pepper shakers for this pattern. However, as mentioned previously, the monax shakers in Newport will serve.

	Pink, Crystal	Plain	CREMAX, MONAX Fired-On Decorations		Pink, Crystal	Plain	CREMAX, MONAX Fired-On Decorations
Bowl, 4½" Cream Soup	4.00	4.50	7.50	Plate, 8" Salad	1.75	3.00	5.00
Bowl, 5¾" Cereal	3.50	4.50	6.50	Plate, 9" Dinner	3.00	3.50	5.50
*Bowl, 8¾" Large Berry	4.00	6.50	12.50	Plate, 11" Salver	4.00	5.00	8.50
Cup	2.50	3.00	4.50	Plate, 12" Salver		6.50	10.00
**Creamer, Footed	2.50	3.50	.6.50	Platter, 13" Oval	5.25	7.25	10.00
Lamp Shade (Many Sizes) $5.00 to $10.00				Saucer	1.25	1.25	1.75
Mustard with Metal Cover				Sherbet, Low Ftd.	7.50		
in Cobalt Blue Only $4.50				**Sherbet, Low Footed	3.00	4.00	6.50
Pitcher, 80 oz. (Crystal				**Sugar, Footed	2.50	3.50	6.50
Decorated Bands)	17.50			Tidbit Servers or Lazy Susans			
Plate, 6" Sherbet	1.25	2.00	2.50	several styles 11.00 to 17.50			
				***Tumblers (Crystal			
				Decorated Bands) 2.50 to 7.50			

*Also in cobalt at 30.00
**Also in cobalt at 17.50
***Several Sizes

141

PRINCESS HOCKING GLASS COMPANY 1931-1935

Colors: Green, 2 yellows, pink; some blue.

In this picture that blue Princess cup and 6″ plate or saucer stand out like diamonds in a coal bin; unfortunately such is not the case in the "real" world! Finding blue Princess is as likely as finding the proverbial "needle in the haystack". There is no way a saucer will ever compare in price to a blue cookie jar; but as a comment on its relative rarity, I owned three blue Princess cookie jars before owning one saucer! A candy dish has also been sighted in this elusive color; so keep your weather eye open. (See the blue cookie jar pictured in the 2nd edition cover photo at back.)

Biggest price jumps were made by the green ash tray, plain relish and dinner plates.

Did you notice that pink footed pitcher in Princess on the cover? The color has a slight orange cast and the design is not all that well defined; but this was true of the green pitcher also. At least we haven't been treated to a pink one with frosted panels down the side like those awful ones that turned up in green---with matching frosted paneled tumblers, yet! Yuk! It won "ugly pitcher of the year" award, hands down though the yellow Cameo milk pitcher which surfaced ran it a close second. No wonder these are uncommon finds; who would have paid good money for them during the 1930's when ready cash was a problem?

An abundance of the common pieces in yellow has tended to overshadow the fact that serving pieces are quite rare. Remember, particularly when ordering something through the mail, to specify which yellow color you want. There are two: one is an amber yellow color known as "apricot"; the other, called "topaz" is a bright yellow color and is usually the one to catch the collector's eye.

People who never heard of Depression Glass often have a green Princess cookie jar in their cabinet. My wife's earliest memories of her grandmother's pantry are of the green Princess cookie jar on the shelf in which they kept honey. When she recalled this for her grandmother it elicited the response, "You mean THAT's Depression Glass?"

	Green	Pink	Yellow Amber		Green	Pink	Yellow Amber
Ash Tray, 4½″	42.50	47.50	47.50	Plate, 11½″, Grill, Closed Handles	5.50	4.00	5.50
Bowl, 4½″ Berry	7.50	5.50	7.50	Plate, 11½″, Sandwich, Handled	6.50	4.50	5.50
Bowl, 5″ Cereal or Oatmeal	9.50	6.50	10.00	Platter, 12″ Closed Handles	8.50	6.50	25.00
Bowl, 9″ Salad, Octagonal	17.50	11.50	37.50	Relish, 7½″, Divided	10.00	7.00	12.50
Bowl, 9½″ Hat Shaped	17.50	12.00	42.50	Relish, 7½″, Plain	30.00		
Bowl, 10″ Oval Vegetable	10.00	9.00	27.50	Salt and Pepper, Pr., 4½″	27.50	22.50	37.50
Butter Dish and Cover	52.50	57.50	375.00	Spice Shakers, Pr. 5½″	17.50		
Cake Stand, 10″	9.50	9.00		Saucer (Same as Sherbet Plate)	2.50	2.00	2.00
†††Candy Dish and Cover	27.50	22.50		Sherbet, Footed	9.00	8.00	19.50
Coaster	15.00	12.00	22.50	Sugar	4.50	3.50	5.50
†Cookie Jar and Cover	20.00	17.50		Sugar Cover	6.00	5.50	7.50
Creamer, Oval	5.50	4.50	7.50	Tumbler, 3″, 5 oz. Juice	12.50	9.50	12.50
††Cup	5.00	3.50	4.00	Tumbler, 4″, 9 oz. Water	12.00	9.50	12.50
Pitcher, 6″, 37 oz.	20.00	15.50	250.00	Tumbler, 5¼″, 13 oz. Iced Tea	15.00	12.00	15.00
Pitcher, 7 3/8″, 24 oz. Footed	375.00	295.00		Tumbler, 4¾″, 9 oz. Sq. Ft.	37.50	35.00	
Pitcher, 8″, 60 oz.	27.50	22.50	40.00	Tumbler, 5¼″, 10 oz. Footed	14.50	10.50	12.50
Plate, 5½″, Sherbet	2.50	2.00	2.50	Tumbler, 6½″, Footed, 12½ oz.	29.50	22.50	
Plate, 8″ Salad	5.50	4.50	4.50	Vase, 8″	15.00	13.00	
Plate, 9½″ Dinner	11.00	6.00	6.00				
††Plate, 9½″ Grill	5.50	4.00	4.50				

†Blue — $350.00
††Blue — $45.00
††† — $350.00

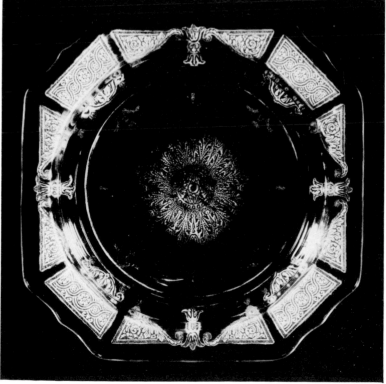

143

QUEEN MARY, (PRISMATIC LINE), "VERTICAL RIBBED"

HOCKING GLASS COMPANY 1936-1940

Colors: Pink, crystal; some ruby red.

Hocking first introduced our Queen Mary pattern as Prismatic Line and the straight lined simplicity of the pattern insured it's popularity at Hocking for almost twenty years as is evidenced by their making a forest green ash tray in it as late as the 1950's.

Based on pricing criteria, this pattern is still affordable in both pink and crystal even though the last year has seen some drastic jumps in a few pieces of pink such as dinner plates and salt and pepper shakers. However, you should know that finding Queen Mary isn't as easy as finding Princess. It will take some patient looking, particularly in pink.

You will find salt shakers in a variety of colors, even amethyst; all colors appear quite common but pink! Shakers come with both metal and red plastic tops as you can see from the picture.

Notice the cigarette jar with the metal cover. This is one of the few patterns to specifically cater to people who smoke!

	Pink, Crystal		Pink, Crystal
Ash Tray, Oval, 2" x 3¾"	2.00	Cup	4.00
Bowl, 4", One Handle or None	2.00	Plate, 6" and 6 5/8"	2.50
Bowls, 5" Berry, 6" Cereal	3.00	Plate, 8½" Salad	3.50
Bowl, 5½", Two Handles	2.50	***Plate, 9¾" Dinner	5.00
Bowl, 7", Small	3.50	Plate, 12" Relish, 3 Sections	5.50
Bowl, 8¾" Large Berry	5.00	Plate, 12" Sandwich	4.50
*Butter Dish or Preserve and Cover	20.00	Plate, 14" Serving Tray	6.50
**Candy Dish and Cover	12.50	Relish Tray, 12", 3 Part	4.50
Candlesticks, 4½", Double Branch, Pr.	8.50	Relish Tray, 14", 4 Part	5.50
Candlesticks, Ruby Red, Pr.	17.50	****Salt and Pepper, Pr.	12.50
Celery or Pickle Dish, 5" x 10"	2.50	Saucer	1.50
Cigarette Jar, Oval, 2" x 3"	4.50	Sherbet, Footed	3.00
Coaster, 3½"	2.00	Sugar, Oval	4.00
Coaster/Ash Tray, 4¼" Square	4.00	Tumbler, 3½", 5 oz. Juice	2.00
Comport, 5¾"	3.00	Tumbler, 4", 9 oz. Water	3.50
Creamer, Oval	4.00	Tumbler, 5", 10 oz. Footed	8.00

*Pink — 75.00
**Pink — 19.00
***Pink — 9.00
****Pink — 35.00

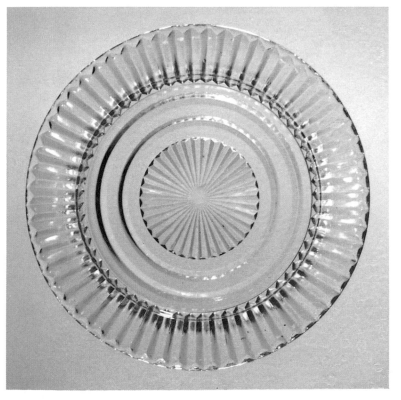

RADIANCE NEW MARTINSVILLE 1936-1939

Colors: Red, cobalt & ice blue, amber, crystal.

As with Moondrops by New Martinsville, Radiance is a better quality glassware, the kind you bought from the department stores rather than that which was given away as premium items. However, having been made in this time period, it is being collected now by some Depression Glass people. The pattern is not found enough to put its popularity at the top of the heap; but those who search do have a diverse number of pieces to help their quest.

Pitcher and butter dishes are considered the important pieces to locate with the handled decanter and 5 piece condiment set running close behind.

The sugar and creamer in this pattern rest on an oval tray; a punch ladle came with the punch bowl set and is now often absent from those sets making it a tough, and desirable, item to happen upon.

On a recent trip I spotted a red lamp with gold decoration. The 12″ flared vase had been drilled as a starting point for this lamp. I've heard of others as well.

You will find pieces trimmed with gold or platinum and it may or may not be attractive. Often the trim is worn which detracts from sales. Should you wish to remove these badly worn trimmings, it can be done with a rust removing agent commonly found in hardware stores. If the trim is in good shape, I'd leave it.

Prices for the Red color Radiance bring 50% to 100% more than those listed below.

	All Colors Except Red		All Colors Except Red
Bon Bon, 6″	5.50	Creamer	6.50
Bon Bon, 6″, Ftd.	6.00	Cruet, Individual	20.00
Bon Bon, 6″, Covered	13.50	Cup	4.50
Bowl, 5″, 2 Handled, Nut	6.50	Decanter, Handled with Stopper	50.00
Bowl, 7″, 2 Part	7.50	Lamp, 12″	35.00
Bowl, 7″, Pickle	6.00	Mayonnaise, 3 Pc. Set	10.00
Bowl, 8″, 3 Part Relish	9.00	Pitcher, 64 Oz.	100.00
Bowl, 10″, Celery	7.50	Plate, 8″ Luncheon	4.00
Bowl, 10″, Crimped	10.00	Plate, 14″, Punch Bowl Liner	15.00
Bowl, 10″, Flared	9.75	Punch Bowl	35.00
Bowl, 12″, Crimped	12.50	Punch Cup	4.00
Bowl, 12″, Flared	12.00	Punch Ladle	40.00
Butter Dish	125.00	Salt & Pepper, Pr.	20.00
Candlestick, 8″, Pr.	15.00	Saucer	2.00
Candle, 2 Light, Pr.	22.50	Sugar	6.50
Cheese and Cracker, 11 Plate Set	13.50	Tray, Oval	15.00
Comport, 5″	6.00	Tumbler, 9 Oz.	8.50
Comport, 6″	7.00	Vase, 10″, Flared	10.00
Condiment Set, 4 Pc. on Tray	85.00	Vase, 12″, Crimped	15.00

RAINDROPS, "OPTIC DESIGN" FEDERAL GLASS COMPANY 1929-1933

Colors: Green, crystal.

Raindrops has the dubious distinction of seldom being discussed except in the connection of is it or isn't it "Thumbprint"/Pear Optic. Even some dealers in the glass tend to confuse the two. Raindrops impressions are rounded little hills or bumps occurring on the **insides** of the pieces and on the undersides of the plates. "Thumbprint"/Pear Optic has elongated or pear shaped impressions which are slightly "scooped out" in the middle.

Someone surely has a mate to this lonely shaker for sale. I've been searching for four years now and have only glimpsed some "not for sale" counterparts in shaker collections. The bumps, again, are on the inside of the shaker.

I still believe the Raindrops sugar lid to be THE rarest lid in Depression Glass. It won't command as big a price as some others due to the pattern having few collectors; and therefore, there is little demand generated for the lid. However, as an example, I've owned nine American Sweetheart monax lids; four pink Mayfair lids and only one Raindrops lid. True, to date, I've only had one yellow Mayfair sugar lid; but I'd almost be willing to gamble that another of those will turn up before the Raindrops. I'm dwelling on this simply to bring home to collectors the fact that simply because something is rare in Depression Glass, it does not necessarily follow that the item will bring a high price. Rarity does not determine price as much as demand does!

	Green		Green
Bowl, 4½" Fruit	2.00	Salt and Pepper, Pr.	37.50
Bowl, 6" Cereal	3.00	Saucer	1.50
Cup	3.00	Sherbet	3.50
Creamer	4.50	Sugar	3.50
Plate, 6" Sherbet	1.50	Sugar Cover	20.00
Plate, 8" Luncheon	2.50	Tumbler, 3", 4 oz.	3.00
		Whiskey, 1 7/8"	3.50

"RIBBON" HAZEL ATLAS GLASS COMPANY Early 1930's

Colors: Green; some black, crystal, pink?

"Ribbon" is another name given by collectors. It's factory "handle" remains in some obscure file. Since the mold is similar to that of Ovide and Cloverleaf, we feel safe in dating the pattern since molds were expensive and were often re-designed for further use.

Several people have told me at various shows in the east that they own pink "Ribbon" shakers. None, however, brought them along to the shows as demonstrative proof.

"Ribbon" is usually sought out by speciality collectors who want the candy dish, sugar and creamer or salt and pepper shakers. Some covet the pieces made in black. Yet, a basic luncheon set is possible in green. It will take time; but it can still be done and without borrowing from the bank!

	Green	Black		Green	Black
Bowl, 4" Berry	2.00		Salt and Pepper, Pr.	15.00	27.50
Bowl, 8" Large Berry	6.00	13.00	Saucer	1.50	
Candy Dish and Cover	20.00		Sherbet, Footed	3.00	
Creamer, Footed	3.50	9.00	Sugar, Footed	3.00	9.00
Cup	2.50		Tumbler, 5½", 10 oz.	5.50	
Plate, 6¼" Sherbet	1.25		Tumbler, 6½", 13 oz.	6.50	
Plate, 8" Luncheon	2.00	8.00			

Please refer to Foreword for pricing information

149

RING, "BANDED RINGS"   HOCKING GLASS COMPANY 1927-1932

Colors: Crystal, crystal w/pink, red, blue, orange, yellow, black, platinum, etc. rings; green, some pink, blue, red.

I want to call to your attention that it is very difficult to collect Ring if you're trying to match the circular bands of color in a precise order. The order of color varies so much that I suggest you be content with whatever you find. Pictured are pieces with yellow, orange, green; yellow, red, orange, black; yellow, red, black; yellow, orange, green, orange green. Hence, wanting a certain order of colors might keep you searching for decades!

Dealers used to buy Ring shakers so they could use the tops for their more prestigious Mayfair shakers. Suddenly, as collectors of the Ring increased, they started searching for Ring shakers for themselves! In the process, it's been discovered that the green Ring shakers are few and far between!

Colors of Ring such as red and Mayfair blue are unusual. Pitcher and tumbler sets are all that have been found in pink. The platinum banded Ring is rather elegant in a setting particularly when accompanied by the stemware.

	Crystal	Crystal Decor. Green		Crystal	Crystal Decor. Green
Bowl, 5" Berry	1.00	1.50	Sandwich Server		
Bowl, 8" Large Berry	3.00	4.50	Center Handle	7.50	15.00
Butter Tub or Ice Bucket	5.50	10.00	Saucer	1.50	2.00
Cocktail Shaker	6.00	12.50	Sherbet, Low		
Cup	2.00	3.00	(for 6½" Plate)	3.50	4.00
Creamer, Footed	2.50	3.50	Sherbet, 4¾" Footed	3.50	5.50
Decanter and Stopper	12.50	20.00	Sugar, Footed	2.50	3.50
Goblet, 7" to 8" (Varies)			Tumbler, 3½", 5 oz.	2.00	3.50
9 oz.	4.50	9.50	Tumbler, 4¼", 9 oz.	2.50	3.00
Ice Tub	7.50	12.50	Tumbler, 5 1/8", 12 oz.	3.00	4.00
Pitcher, 8", 60 oz.	8.50	12.50	Tumbler, 3½", Footed,		
*Pitcher, 8½", 80 oz.	9.50	15.00	Cocktail	3.00	4.00
Plate, 6¼" Sherbet	1.25	2.00	*Tumbler, 5½", Footed,		
Plate, 6", Off Center Ring	2.50	3.50	Water	3.50	4.50
**Plate, 8" Luncheon	1.25	2.50	Tumbler, 6½", Footed,		
***Salt and Pepper, Pr., 3"	10.00	15.00	Iced Tea	4.00	7.50
			Whiskey, 2", 1½ oz.	2.50	4.50

*Also found in Pink. Priced as Green.
**Red — 17.50. Blue — 20.50.
***Green — 52.50.

ROCK CRYSTAL, "EARLY AMERICAN ROCK CRYSTAL"

McKEE GLASS COMPANY 1920's and 1930's in colors.

Colors: Pink, green, cobalt, red, yellow, amber, blue-green, crystal, etc.

The color, variety and beauty of Rock Crystal shown in my last two books has brought several new collectors to this pattern! Many collectors have expressed to me that they hadn't known so many colors existed in the pattern.

Red is the most desirable color to find, but there seem to be three distinct shades of red to be found: a very dark red, a vivid red and an amberina red, having lots of yellow in it. It is discouraging to find a long sought after item only to find it is the wrong shade!

Would you believe that collectors of crystal have a problem with shading also? Some crystal has a tint of purple; later pieces have better clarity. You must realize that crystal dates as far back as the early 1900's and that until 1915 each piece was marked "press cut". There will be additional pieces found in crystal than those listed here. This listing should, however, include most of the colored items manufactured. I have heard rumors of a red butter dish; but as yet, I have not confirmed such an item to exist.

The large 64 oz. scalloped edge pitcher is shown on the cover in green and here in crystal. Next to it is the small quart pitcher having the same shape. Notice the 8¼" tankard on the other side.

The butter dish and a 14" punch bowl in crystal have most people searching. Cobalt blue items in Rock Crystal seem to be limited to the 2 lite candelabra and a 12½" center piece bowl that is footed.

For pricing purposes, the colors are divided into three columns. However, colors of Rock Crystal include: four shades of green, aquamarine, vaseline yellow, amber, pink and satin frosted pink, red slag, red, amberina red, crystal, frosted crystal, crystal with goofus decoration, crystal with gold decoration, amethyst, milkglass, blue frosted or "Jap" blue, and cobalt blue.

Happy hunting!

	Crystal	Green Amber Pink	Red & Other Colors
Bon Bon, 7½", S.E.	6.00	12.00	17.50
Bowl, 4", S.E.	3.00	5.00	9.00
Bowl, 4½", S.E.	3.50	6.00	10.00
Bowl, 5", S.E.	4.50	7.00	12.50
**Bowl, 5" Finger Bowl with 7" Plate, P.E.	8.00	12.50	20.00
Bowl, 7" Pickle or Spoon Tray	8.00	14.00	22.50
Bowl, 7", Salad, S.E.	6.50	9.00	15.00
Bowl, 8", Salad, S.E.	7.50	10.00	15.00
Bowl, 9", Salad, S.E.	8.50	14.00	22.50
Bowl, 10½", Salad, S.E.	10.00	15.00	27.50
Bowl, 11½" Two Part Relish	9.00	15.00	25.00
Bowl, 12" Oblong Celery	12.50	17.50	27.50
***Bowl, 12½" Footed Center Bowl	25.00	45.00	97.50
Bowl, 13" Roll Tray	15.00	20.00	37.50
Bowl, 14" Six Part Relish	15.00	27.50	65.00
Butter Dish and Cover	167.50		
Candelabra, Two Lite Pr.	15.00	20.00	39.50
Candelabra, Three Lite Pr.	17.50	25.00	49.50

Rock Crystal Prices Continued on Page 154.

153

	Crystal	Green Amber Pink	Red & Other Colors
Candlestick, 5½" Low, Pr.	12.50	17.50	32.50
Candlestick, 8½" Tall, Pr.	37.50	47.50	67.50
Candy and Cover, Round	15.00	35.00	75.00
Cake Stand, 11", Footed, 2¾" High	12.00	20.00	42.50
Comport, 7"	9.00	12.50	22.50
Creamer, Flat, S.E.	9.50		
Creamer, 9 oz., Footed	7.50	12.50	20.00
Cruet and Stopper, 6 oz. Oil	35.00	47.50	67.50
Cup, 7 oz.	6.50	10.00	19.50
Goblet, 7½ oz., 8 oz. Low Footed	9.00	16.00	27.50
Goblet, 11 oz., Low Footed, Iced Tea	10.00	17.00	29.00
Jelly, 5" Footed, S.E.	9.00	11.00	20.00
Lamp, Electric	40.00	79.00	150.00
Parfait, 3½ oz., Low Footed	5.00		
Pitcher, Qt., S.E.	25.00	47.50	
Pitcher, ½ Gal., 7½" High	50.00	95.00	
Pitcher Large, 9" Covered	67.50	97.50	157.50
Plate, 6" Bread and Butter, S.E.	2.25	3.50	6.00
Plate, 7½", P.E. & S.E.	3.00	4.50	12.50
Plate, 8½", P.E. & S.E.	5.00	6.50	15.00
Plate, 9", S.E.	7.00	8.50	18.00
Plate, 10½", S.E.	15.00	12.50	22.40
Plate, 11½", S.E.	12.00	15.00	20.00
Plate, 10½" Dinner, S.E. (large center design)	12.50	15.00	22.00
Punch Bowl and Stand, 14"	225.00		
Salt and Pepper (2 styles)	35.00	47.50	
Salt Dip	17.50		
Sandwich Server Center Handled	12.00	17.50	50.00
Saucer	3.00	4.00	6.00
Sherbet or Egg, 3½ oz., Footed	7.50	11.00	18.00
Spooner	17.50		
Stemware, 1 oz., Footed Cordial	9.00	15.00	25.00
Stemware, 2 oz. Wine	6.50	12.50	22.50
Stemware, 3 oz. Wine	8.50	15.00	25.00
Stemware, 3½" oz., Footed Cocktail	7.00	12.50	25.00
Stemware, 6 oz., Footed Champagne	7.50	12.50	22.50
Stemware, 8 oz, Large Footed Goblet	9.00	17.50	32.50
Sundae, 6 oz. Low Footed	7.00	12.50	22.50
Sugar, 10 oz. Open	7.00	12.50	22.00
Sugar, 10 oz. Covered	20.00	30.00	45.00
Syrup with Lid	37.50		
Tumbler, 2½" oz., Whiskey	6.00	12.00	29.00
Tumbler, 5 oz. Juice	8.00	10.00	22.50
Tumbler, 5 oz., Old Fashioned	9.00	12.00	25.00
Tumbler, 9 oz., Concave or Straight	9.00	12.00	22.50
Tumbler, 12 oz., Concave or Straight	12.00	15.00	30.00
Vase, Cornucopia	17.50	25.00	
Vase, 11" Footed	20.00	35.00	77.50

*S.E. McKee designation for scalloped edge
**P.E. McKee designation for plain edge
***Red Slag — $300.00. Cobalt — $137.50

Please refer to Foreword for pricing information

155

ROSE CAMEO BELMONT TUMBLER COMPANY 1931

Color: Green.

Although the patent to Rose Cameo is registered to the Belmont Tumbler Company, there are strong indications that the glass itself may have been manufactured at the Hazel Atlas Plant.

There is one style of tumbler missing from the photograph; otherwise, what you see is all you may have. The edge of the other style tumbler flares outward.

When ordering this, you need to specify you want the pattern with the rose inside the cameo. Some people still confuse this with Cameo pattern which has the dancing girl figure within the design.

I once excitedly ordered an ice tub in Rose Cameo thinking I was discovering a new piece to the pattern. I got Cameo---which, of course, was not a total loss!

	Green		Green
Bowl, 4½" Berry	2.50	Sherbet	3.00
Bowl, 5" Cereal	3.50	Tumbler, 5", Footed (2 Styles)	6.50
Plate, 7" Salad	3.50		

ROSEMARY, "DUTCH ROSE" FEDERAL GLASS COMPANY 1935-1937

Colors: Amber, pink, green.

Rosemary has a "history". This is the pattern that ultimately came from Federal's twice changing of its Mayfair pattern after learning that Hocking had beaten them to the patent office with the name "Mayfair".

You will notice that the Rosemary pattern does not have the arches around the base which the "transitional" Mayfair pieces have; nor does it have the arches and waffling around the base that regular Federal Mayfair has; Rosemary has perfectly plain glass at the base of its pieces save for the center rose motif.

Amber is the most plentiful color in Rosemary; so, naturally, pink and green are most in demand. Pink supplies seem to be dwindling faster than the green.

Rosemary sports a handleless sugar bowl; this piece causes more consternation with new collectors than any other. It's not a tumbler and it's not a sherbet. It's the sugar bowl!

Bowls (cream soup, oval vegetable, cereal) seem the hardest items to locate; next come tumblers.

	Amber	Pink/ Green		Amber	Pink/ Green
Bowl, 5" Berry	2.00	4.00	Plate, Dinner	3.50	8.50
Bowl, 5" Cream Soup	6.00	10.00	Plate, Grill	3.50	5.50
Bowl, 6" Cereal	5.00	8.00	Platter, 12" Oval	6.00	9.00
Bowl, 10" Oval Vegetable	6.50	10.00	Saucer	1.25	2.00
Creamer, Footed	5.50	7.50	Sugar, Footed	5.50	7.50
Cup	3.00	4.50	Tumbler, 4¼", 9 oz.	7.50	10.50
Plate, 6¾" Salad	2.00	2.50			

ROULETTE, "MANY WINDOWS"   HOCKING GLASS COMPANY 1935-1939

Colors: Pink, green.

Did you know that if you "roulette" something you mark it with a series of incisions? Obviously the prim little old lady who renamed her pattern "Many Windows" so she wouldn't have to tell her friends it was called Roulette didn't.

Collectors of the pattern inform me that though the listing of tumblers is lengthy, in actual fact they are not so numerous. I've also had one lady tell me to not make the pattern sound too interesting as she hasn't gotten all hers yet and she doesn't want any more competition!

Please notice the pitcher in this pattern. The rouletted design occurs about two-thirds the way up the side as it does in the glasses. There is another pitcher around having a similar cubed effect around the bottom of the pitcher. When the design occurs at the bottom, it isn't Roulette pattern.

Too, there is a cobalt tumbler which has an embossed rather than an impressed design which resembles Roulette; it's a maverick and does not belong with Roulette.

	Pink, Green, Crystal
Bowl, 9" Fruit	7.50
Cup	3.25
Pitcher, 8", 64 oz.	17.50
Plate, 6" Sherbet	1.25
Plate, 8½" Luncheon	3.25
Plate, 12" Sandwich	4.00
Saucer	1.75
Sherbet	3.00
Tumbler, 3¼", 5 oz. Juice	3.75
Tumbler, 3¼", 7½ oz. Old Fashioned	5.50
Tumbler, 4 1/8", 9 oz. Water	4.50
Tumbler, 5 1/8", 12 oz. Iced Tea	8.50
Tumbler, 5½", 10 oz. Footed	7.50
Whiskey, 2½", 1½ oz.	5.50

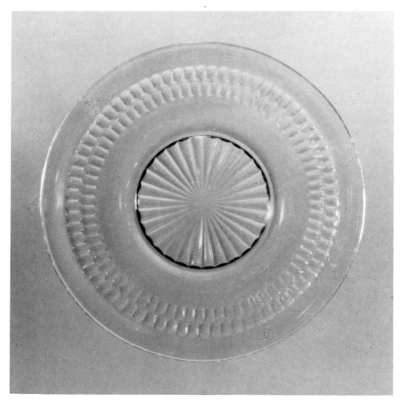

159

"ROUND ROBIN"   MANUFACTURER UNKNOWN Probably early 1930's

Colors: Green, iridescent.

There is little action in "Round Robin" as there are relatively few pieces and they are seldom seen. A few people have told me they were attempting to put together luncheon sets but that they were relying mostly on the flea markets and the mail to do so. Dealers seldom take "Round Robin" to shows. If you collect it, make a point to ask the dealers for it; once someone requests something, they generally start looking for it.

I'm using the same picture here as was in the last book. Again, I apologize for showing two creamers and no sugar. Refer to the first or second edition book for a picture of the sugar bowl; and yes, hawk eyes, I know the green creamer has a chip on it; but I felt fortunate to find even that!

	Green	Iridescent		Green	Iridescent
Bowl, 4" Berry	1.50	2.00	Plate, 8" Luncheon	2.00	2.50
Cup, Footed	2.50	2.50	Plate, 12" Sandwich	3.50	4.00
Creamer, Footed	4.00	4.50	Saucer	1.25	1.50
Domino Tray	15.00		Sherbet	3.50	4.00
Plate, 6" Sherbet	1.25	1.25	Sugar	4.00	4.50

ROXANA   HAZEL ATLAS GLASS COMPANY 1932

Colors: Yellow, white, crystal.

I am still of the conviction that Roxana and Bowknot should be married. With Bowknot's saucerless cup and Roxana's cupless saucer, it should be an ideal match.

I have met a few ladies who collect this because its their namesake. Otherwise, I suspect that writers of books are the only other people who ever seek it---not because it isn't an attractive little pattern, but because there's so very little of it!

The sherbet is footed but not stemmed. One was pictured in my first and second editions.

	Yellow	White		Yellow
Bowl, 4½" x 2 3/8"	4.50	10.00	Plate, 6" Sherbet	2.50
Bowl, 5" Berry	3.50		Saucer	2.00
Bowl, 6" Cereal	4.00		Sherbet, Footed	3.00
			Tumbler, 4", 9 oz.	5.00

ROYAL LACE HAZEL ATLAS GLASS COMPANY 1934-1941

Colors: Pink, green, crystal, blue, amethyst.

The demand for cobalt blue Royal Lace is being felt once again in the trade; for a time, it was stymied by collectors turning to the other colors, ostensibly because the prices for the blue had gotten too out of line with the actual supply of it. When prices in the other colors began to catch up, or exceed, those of cobalt, then it became desirable once more.

More people collecting the crystal is beginning to cause a shortage in some pieces of that color. Generally speaking, crystal and pink prices run about the same save for the butter dish which is rather plentiful as compared with the extremely scarce pink one! You'll find green or blue butter dishes before you'll find the pink, though the prices do not mirror this at present.

Remember to check the inside rims of the plates, bowls and butter bottoms for chips. Possibly they originally came from the molds with this roughness; if not that, then the stacking of these pieces in cabinets over the years is our culprit!

To date, that toddy set is the only item to appear in the amethyst color except for sherbet in metal holder. This set comes in blue, also; missing from the picture here is the ladle with the red knob on the end which matches the knob on the metal lid. This set originally sold for $.98. At least, that was the price sticker on one received as a gift in 1938.

Speaking of original ads, I have one from the 1930's featuring cobalt Moderntone and cobalt Royal Lace side by side. For $2.99 you could become the proud owner of FORTY-FOUR pieces!

	Crystal Pink	Green	Blue	Amethyst
Bowl, 4¾" Cream Soup	7.50	19.50	13.50	
Bowl, 5" Berry	9.00	12.50	12.50	
Bowl, 10" Round Berry	9.50	15.00	22.50	
Bowl, 10", 3 Leg, Straight Edge	11.00	25.00	27.50	
Bowl, 10", 3 Leg, Rolled Edge	12.50	47.50	45.00	
Bowl, 10", 3 Leg, Ruffled Edge	13.50	27.50	35.00	
Bowl, 11" Oval Vegetable	8.50	14.50	19.50	
*Butter Dish and Cover	85.00	200.00	245.00	
Candlestick, Pr., Straight Edge	15.00	27.50	45.00	
Candlestick, Pr., Rolled Edge	17.50	37.50	47.50	
Candlestick, Pr., Ruffled Edge	19.50	40.00	45.00	
Cookie Jar and Cover	25.00	32.50	117.50	
Cream, Footed	6.50	10.50	15.00	
Cup	4.50	7.50	12.00	
Pitcher, 54 oz., Straight Sides	32.50	57.50	62.50	
Pitcher, 8", 68 oz.	32.50	67.50	77.50	
Pitcher, 8", 86 oz.	37.50	87.50	92.50	
Pitcher, 8½", 96 oz.	42.50	97.50	102.50	
Plate, 6" Sherbet	2.50	3.50	4.50	
Plate, 8½" Luncheon	3.50	6.50	10.50	
Plate, 10" Dinner	5.50	9.00	13.50	
Plate, 9 7/8" Grill	5.50	9.00	12.50	
Platter, 13" Oval	9.50	17.50	22.50	
Salt and Pepper, Pr.	32.50	70.00	117.50	
Saucer	2.50	3.50	4.00	
Sherbet, Footed	5.50	12.50	15.00	
Sherbet in Metal Holder	3.50		12.00	20.00
Sugar	5.50	8.50	14.00	
Sugar Lid	9.50	17.50	30.00	
Tumbler, 3½", 5 oz.	7.50	15.50	16.00	
Tumbler, 4 1/8", 9 oz.	7.50	14.50	15.00	
Tumbler, 4 7/8", 12 oz.	10.00	16.00	22.00	
Tumbler, 5 3/8", 13 oz.	11.50	17.00	22.50	
Toddy or Cider Set: Includes Cookie Jar, Metal Lid, Metal Tray, 8 Roly-Poly Cups and Ladle			75.00	87.50

*Butter Dish in Crystal — $42.50

Please refer to Foreword for pricing information

162

Factory experimental plate.

163

ROYAL RUBY   ANCHOR HOCKING GLASS COMPANY 1939-1960's; 1977

Color: Red.

Royal Ruby refers solely to the red glassware made by Anchor Hocking. Their initial promotion started in 1938. Some people tend to throw all red glassware into the Royal Ruby category regardless of what company made it. Strictly speaking, Royal Ruby was the term coined by Anchor Hocking to describe the red glassware issued during its late 30's early 40's Royal Ruby Promotion.

Anchor Hocking's idea to re-introduce some pieces of this in 1977 was obviously not the best news collectors of the glass had heard. Supposedly, these later pieces were marked by the anchor trademark of the company; not all have been so marked, I understand. There are differences between old and new. The new is lighter in weight for one thing and the color does not quite have the rich redness of the earlier pieces. Their catalogue lists the following pieces as having been made in '77: Bubble, 4½" and 8" bowls; plain tumblers in 7, 9, 12 and 16 oz. sizes; an ivy ball vase; a punch cup and a square ash tray. These are probably prominently displayed at your local dish barn; so drop by and take a look. Remember, I said, "Look". If the item remains unpopular, maybe they won't make more! Don't laugh; that theory apparently worked with the "Recollection" Madrid! Federal is no longer in business.

The squared items you find in red are a 1950's issue which came along about the same time as the "Forest Green" pieces with the same shape.

Serving pieces and stemware items have been quickly gobbled up. Most often seen pieces today are the vases.

	Red
Ash Tray, 4½" Square	2.50
Bowl, 4¼" Berry	3.00
Bowl, 7½" Soup	7.50
Bowl, 8" Oval Vegetable	8.50
Bowl, 8½" Large Berry	8.00
Creamer, Flat	4.50
Creamer, Footed	5.50
Cup (Round or Square)	3.00
Goblet, Ball Stem	7.50
Lamp	17.50
Pitcher, 42 oz., Tilted or Upright	15.00
Pitcher, 3 qt., Tilted	35.00
Pitcher, 3 qt., Upright	20.00
Plate, 6½" Sherbet	1.50
Plate, 7" Salad	2.50
Plate, 7¾" Luncheon	3.00
Plate, 9" or 9¼" Dinner	5.00
Punch Bowl and Stand	27.50
Punch Cup	2.50
Saucer (Round or Square)	1.50
Sherbet, Footed	4.50
Sugar, Flat	4.50
Sugar, Footed	5.50
Tumbler, 3½ oz. Cocktail	5.50
Tumbler, 5 oz., Juice, 2 Styles	4.00
Tumbler, 9 oz. Water	4.00
Tumbler, 10 oz. Water	4.50
Tumbler, 13 oz. Iced Tea	6.50
Tumbler, 2½ oz. Footed Wine	6.50
Vase, 4" Ball Shaped	3.50
Vase, 6½" Bulbous, Tall	7.50
Vases, Several Styles (Small)	5.00
Vases, Several Styles (Large)	8.50

165

"S" PATTERN, "STRIPED ROSE BAND"

MACBETH EVANS GLASS COMPANY 1930-1933

Colors: Crystal; crystal w/trims of platinum, blue, green, amber; pink, some amber, green, red and white.

Confession is supposedly good for the soul, so I'll admit I goofed when I wrote the text for this last time---some months after the actual photographs were taken. I looked at the photograph and wrote about the "orchid" trim, having totally forgotten about the trim on those pieces being a rich light blue. When dealers began looking for "orchid" and then coming back and saying all they could find was blue, I had egg on my face. (I don't know what that makes my plagerist have on his---since he copied that, too! Oh, well; if you're going to copy a good book, you may as well copy its mistakes, also; that way YOUR ignorance doesn't show--- or does it?) Anyway, what happened to cause the pretty blue to look "orchid" was our inclusion of the red "S" plate; the camera picked up its rosy hued reflection and bounced it back to the rest of the glass, turning the blue to orchid. You'll notice that the amber pieces even have a rosey glow about them.

I thought the 6" monax sherbet plate was an interesting find. Then I saw a fired-on white plate at a show I attended. After seeing that, I realized just how pretty my monax sherbet plate was! It's thin edge dances out to show fire when held to light. The same thing can be said about the fired-on red as opposed to the true cherry red; "true" color is best!

The tid-bit server here is original. The bottom was made from the cake plate. However, I've sworn off listing tid bits since people started "assembling" them. Possibly this cake plate costs enough to make that practice prohibitive in this pattern; but you never know. Before you get shook, I omitted it from the 3rd edition and not one person questioned it.

Silk screen process was tried on both crystal and green "S" Pattern pitchers. The pattern was not molded into the glass but applied to the outside of the pitcher through a process called "silk-screening". Most pitchers found have the design molded into the glass.

	Yellow, Amber, Crystal	Crystal With Trims
*Bowl, 5½" Cereal	2.00	3.00
Bowl, 8½" Large Berry	4.00	5.50
*Creamer, Thick or Thin	3.50	5.00
*Cup, Thick or Thin	2.00	3.00
Pitcher, 80 oz. (Like "Dogwood") (Green: 300.00)	32.50	37.50
Pitcher, 80 oz. (Like "American Sweetheart")	42.50	47.50
Plate, 6" Sherbet (Monax: 14.00)	1.25	1.50
**Plate, 8" Luncheon	2.00	2.50
Plate, 9¼" Dinner	2.50	4.00
Plate Grill	2.50	4.50
Plate, 11" Heavy Cake	25.00	27.50
Plate, 13" Heavy Cake	42.50	37.50
*Saucer	1.25	1.50
Sherbet, Low Footed	3.00	4.50
*Sugar, Thick and Thin	3.00	5.00
Tumbler, 3½", 5 oz.	2.50	4.50
Tumbler, 4", 9 oz. (Green: 37.50)	3.00	5.00
Tumbler, 4¼", 10 oz.	3.50	5.50
Tumbler, 5", 12 oz.	4.50	6.00

*Fired-on red items will run approximately three times price of amber.
**Deep Red — $62.50.

Please refer to Foreword for pricing information

SANDWICH HOCKING GLASS COMPANY 1939-1964; 1977

Unfortunately, Anchor Hocking decided to get into the re-issue business by making a Sandwich cookie jar once again. However, it's easy to tell the new from the old; the newer version went "deluxe".

		New	Old
Cookie Jar:	Height	10¼"	9¼"
	Opening Width	5½"	4 7/8"
	Circumference/Largest Part	22"	19"

Dinner plates in both crystal and green have taken leaps in prices; other pieces have held steady. However, I might suggest that since the green dinner plates have increased in price so much, it could well portend an increase in the sugar, creamer, cup and saucer in green.

For those of you who didn't get the 3rd edition I will repeat the reasoning for the seeming dearth of the larger green pitcher in Sandwich. Five pieces of green Sandwich were used as a premium item in a certain brand of oats. Among those items were the juice glasses and tumblers. Since this was prior to "instant" cereals, practically everyone had a set of glasses. However, someone tried to market the pitcher and glasses as a set. Everyone had the glasses already; so American frugality prevailed and the pitcher sets sat on merchant's shelves. They didn't sell. It's possible that some may still be packed away in warehouses somewhere by merchants who invested too heavily; but, to date, the half gallon pitcher is scarcely seen in our market.

I'm often asked about the price for the opaque white punch bowl or egg nog sets. In my area, Kentucky, top price is $20 to $25 if you can locate someone who wants one. Ashland oil sold them for $1.79 or $1.89 with oil change and lube and they are easily found here. They come, also, with a gold trim.

The small custard liner in green was one of the premium items found in oats; so it's plentiful. However, that same liner located in crystal is considered to be "a find".

Where are the green cookie jar lids? One of the factory workers seems to recall that that item was promoted (sans lid) as a vase.

Hocking made:

				Red	1950's-1960's
Crystal	1930-1960's	Pink	1939-1940	Forest Green	1950's-1960's
Amber (Desert Gold)	1960's	Royal Ruby	1939-1940	White (opaque)	1950's

	Crystal	Desert Gold	Ruby Red	Forest Green	Pink		Crystal	Desert Gold	Forest Green
Bowl, 4 7/8" Berry	1.50	2.50	8.50	1.25	2.50	Pitcher, 6" Juice	32.50		62.50
Bowl, 6" Cereal	5.00	5.00				Pitcher, ½ gal., Ice Lip	37.50		132.50
Bowl, 6½" Smooth						Plate, 7" Dessert	4.00	2.00	
or Scalloped	3.50	4.00		12.50		Plate, 9" Dinner	7.00	3.00	27.50
Bowl, 7" Salad	4.00			17.50		Plate, 9" Indent			
Bowl, 8" Smooth						For Punch Cup	2.50		
or Scalloped	3.50		22.50	22.50	7.50	Plate, 12" Sandwich	4.50	6.50	
Bowl, 8¼" Oval	3.50					Saucer	1.25	2.00	3.25
Butter Dish, Low	25.00					Sherbet, Footed	3.50		
Cookie Jar and Cover	22.50	25.00		16.00†		Sugar and Cover	5.50		12.50†
Creamer	2.50			12.50		Tumbler, 5 oz. Juice	2.00		1.50
Cup, Tea or Coffee	1.50	3.50		10.00		Tumbler, 9 oz. Water	4.00		2.50
Custard Cup	1.50			1.00		Tumbler, 9 oz. Footed	5.50		
Custard Cup Liner	4.25			1.00					

†(No Cover)

169

SANDWICH INDIANA GLASS COMPANY 1920's-1970's

Colors: Crystal, amber, pink, red, teal blue, light green.   *(See Reproduction Section)*

What? You just read about Sandwich. Yes, you did. There are two of them here, each made by a different company. So when ordering, specify which company's Sandwich pattern you need.

My inclination is to lower prices drastically in crystal; however, since some people have an investment to consider I won't. You collectors for the crystal need to be aware that there is more new Sandwich floating around now than the old compliments of Tiara Home Products. **Please refer to the section on reproductions** for samples and descriptions of what else is being made by Indiana for the Tiara Company. Especially notice the light amber pictured here as opposed to the deeper amber pictured in the back.

I can vouch for three items in red Sandwich dating from 1933 i.e. cups, creamers and sugars. May we assume a saucer accompanied the cup? I know this because these specific items are found with inscriptions for the 1933 World's Fair. However, in 1969, Tiara Home Products produced red pitchers, 9 oz. goblets, cups, saucers, wines, wine decanter, 13" serving tray, creamers, sugars and salad and dinner plates. Now if your pieces glow yellow under a black light or if you KNOW that your Aunt Sophie held her red dishes in her lap while fording the swollen stream in a buggy, then I'd say your red Sandwich pieces are old. Other than that, I know of no way to tell if they are or aren't. NO, I won't even say that all old red glass glows. I know SOME of it does because of a certain type of process they used. I've even seen some newer glass glow; but Tiara's 1969 red Sandwich glass does not.

The tid bit tray consists of the 10½" plate and the top is Indiana's 6" hexagonal nappy.

Where did the crystal butter tops go? I've found several drilled with holes to be used as "globes" for metal ceiling fixtures.

Crystal	Late 1920's-today	Pink	Late 1920's-early 1930's	Teal Blue 1950's
Amber	Late 1920's-1970's	Red	1933-1970's	Lt. Green 1930's

	Crystal	Pink/ Green	Teal Blue	Red
Ash Tray Set (Club, Spade, Heart, Diamond Shapes)	8.50	12.50		
Bowl, 4¼" Berry	1.50	3.00		
Bowl, 6"	2.50	3.50		
Bowl, 6", 6 Sides	3.00		4.50	
Bowl, 8¼"	4.50	8.50		
Bowl, 9" Console	7.00	14.50		
Bowl, 10" Console	7.00	17.50		
Butter Dish and Cover, Domed	62.50	125.00	177.50	
Candlesticks, 3½", Pr.	8.50	12.50		
Candlesticks, 7", Pr.	17.50	27.50		
Creamer	3.50	6.50		25.00
Cruet, 6½ oz. and Stopper	37.50		97.50	
Cup	2.50	4.00	4.50	20.00
Creamer and Sugar on Diamond Shaped Tray	12.50		20.00	
Decanter and Stopper	32.50	62.50		
Goblet, 9 oz.	8.50	12.50		
Pitcher, 68 oz.	42.50	77.50		
Plate, 6" Sherbet	1.25	2.50	3.00	
Plate, 7" Bread and Butter	2.00	3.50		
Plate, 8" Oval, Indent for Sherbet	3.00	5.00	6.50	
Plate, 8 3/8" Luncheon	2.50	4.50		
Plate, 10½" Dinner	6.50	12.00		
Plate, 13" Sandwich	7.50	12.00		
Sandwich Server, Center Handle	17.50	22.50		
Saucer	1.50	2.50	2.50	5.00
Sherbet, 3¼"	3.50	4.50	4.50	
Sugar, Large Open	3.50	7.50		25.00
Tumbler, 3 oz. Footed Cocktail	10.50	12.50		
Tumbler, 8 oz. Footed Water	9.50	10.00		
Tumbler, 12 oz. Footed Iced Tea	15.00	21.50		
Wine, 3", 4 oz.	9.50	17.50		

171

SHARON, "CABBAGE ROSE" FEDERAL GLASS COMPANY 1935-1939

Colors: Pink, green, amber; some crystal.   *(See Reproduction Section)*

Sharon was never made in blue---by Federal Glass Company. Why that curious beginning? A private individual has made blue butter and cheese dishes (among other colors) which closely resemble our dear Sharon. However, people with old cheese and butter dishes need not worry about the value of their piece being substantiated. The new dishes are readily distinguished from the old. All this influx did was to fill gaps, however unorthodoxly, for people who never hoped to own the Sharon cheese and butter dishes---and who still don't technically. They have the sham; the stop-gap; and most of them are wholly cognizant of the basic worthlessness of what they have. They say they don't care since it filled the space in their set. The trouble only comes when some fast buck artist dupes some unsuspecting soul into parting with too many dollars. Know your glass before you buy. (By the way, $20 is a very high price to pay for these reproductions; half that would be more realistic!) You can learn all you need to know to **avoid being duped by studying the information given at the back of this book in the section on reproductions**.

For novices I repeat the difference between the legitimate butter and cheese dishes. The tops for the two dishes are the same; it's the bottoms you need to notice. The butter bottom was made from the 1½" deep jam dish onto which they made a tiny ledge of glass for the butter top to rest around. This ridge is so tiny in most cases that if you tried to scoot the butter dish across the table using the knob, you'd scoot the top off the butter bottom. The cheese dish was made by adding a rim to the salad plate INTO WHICH the dish top would fit. The cheese dish ridge remains outside of the top once the top is placed on the dish. You can see the glass ridge if you look closely at the amber cheese dish in the picture. The pink covered dish is the butter dish. (The 1½" high jam dish sits behind the green shakers. The 2" high soup bowl sits behind the pink shakers; beginners confuse these, also.)

All prices for all colors of this pattern are presently in an upward spiral with soup bowls, cheese and jam dishes taking off like shooting stars!

Green Sharon footed iced teas do exist; I've had six! Footed amber iced teas are only slightly less difficult to find than green. Amber Sharon, in general, is harder to find than pink; yet today's prices don't reflect this.

	Amber	Pink	Green
Bowl, 5" Berry	3.25	4.50	5.50
Bowl, 5" Cream Soup	8.50	15.00	17.50
Bowl, 6" Cereal	5.50	9.00	9.50
Bowl, 7½", Flat Soup Two Inches Deep	10.50	13.50	
Bowl, 8½" Large Berry	3.50	7.50	12.00
Bowl, 9½" Oval Vegetable	5.50	9.50	12.00
Bowl, 10½" Fruit	10.00	12.50	18.50
Butter Dish and Cover	30.00	35.00	62.50
Cake Plate, Footed, 11½"	13.50	15.00	37.50
Candy Jar and Cover	20.00	25.00	97.50
Cheese Dish and Cover	127.50	450.00	
Creamer, Footed	5.00	7.50	9.00
Cup	4.00	5.00	6.00
Jam Dish, 7½"	22.50	57.50	25.00
Pitcher, 80 oz., With or Without Ice Lip	72.50	69.50	267.50
Plate, 6" Bread and Butter	2.00	2.50	3.00
Plate, 7½" Salad	6.50	9.50	9.50
Plate, 9½" Dinner	6.00	7.50	9.00
Platter, 12½" Oval	6.50	8.50	12.00
Salt and Pepper, Pr.	22.50	32.50	50.00
Saucer	2.00	3.50	3.50
Sherbet, Footed	6.00	6.50	15.00
Sugar	4.00	6.50	8.50
Sugar Lid	12.50	12.50	20.00
Tumbler, 4 1/8", 9 oz. Thick or Thin	11.50	15.00	27.50
Tumbler, 5¼", 12 oz. Thick or Thin	15.00	17.50	37.50
Tumbler, 6½", Footed, 15 oz.	35.00	23.50	97.50

173

SIERRA, "PINWHEEL" JEANNETTE GLASS COMPANY 1931-1933

Colors: Pink, green.

Spanish speaking people will recognize the name for this pattern as their word for saw; and if you look at the pattern shot for the plate, you can certainly see the resemblance to our modern day circular saw blades.

There are a couple of oddities in Sierra. First, the cup, tumbler and pitcher of the pattern all have smooth, rather than serrated, edges. Why? I should imagine it makes for considerably less spillage that way---otherwise you'd have the 1930's version of today's prankster's dribble glasses. The second irregularity is what is called the "Adam-Sierra" butter dish. See the pink butter dish pictured? If you look closely, you see the Adam pattern motif imprinted on the outside while the saw-toothed Sierra pattern is molded on the inside of the butter dish.

Sierra is one of the few patterns in which the sugar lid sells for less than the sugar. The reason is obvious. It had no sharp pointed edges to get knocked off. Mint condition Sierra pattern is a problem because of its design.

Green pitchers and tumblers all seem to be in hiding.

Watch your cups when buying. Some people tend to sit any paneled cup atop a Sierra saucer. It must have the saw-tooth serrations before the clear rim!

	Pink	Green		Pink	Green
Bowl, 5½" Cereal	4.50	5.50	Plate, 9" Dinner	4.50	6.00
Bowl, 8½" Large Berry	8.00	8.50	Platter, 11" Oval	9.00	9.50
Bowl, 9¼" Oval Vegetable	12.00	15.00	Salt and Pepper, Pr.	20.00	25.00
Butter Dish and Cover	37.50	40.00	Saucer	2.50	2.50
Creamer	7.50	9.50	Serving Tray, 2 Handles	6.00	6.50
Cup	5.00	6.00	Sugar	6.00	6.00
Pitcher, 6½", 32 oz.	27.50	52.50	Sugar Cover	5.00	6.00
			Tumbler, 4½", 9 oz. Footed	12.50	17.50

SPIRAL HOCKING GLASS COMPANY 1928-1930

Colors: Green.

New to the business and extremely knowledgeable, I would blithely tell everyone that the difference between Hocking's Spiral and Imperial's Twisted Optic was the direction of the spirals. Hocking's went left, or with the clock; Imperial's went right, or counterclockwise. IN GENERAL, that's true. Yet, Imperial's candy jar appears to go left---unless you turn it upside down; and Spiral's center handled server goes right---unless you look through the bottom! The difference is relatively unimportant, except to purists, in these minor patterns. Dealers tend to lump all companies's spiraling patterns together anyway as "one of those spiraling patterns", thus broadening your range of choice.

Some people are gathering luncheon sets in this because its inexpensive.

	Green		Green
Bowl, 4¾" Berry	2.00	Plate, 8" Luncheon	2.00
Bowl, 7" Mixing	3.00	Preserve and Cover	12.50
Bowl, 8" Large Berry	4.50	Salt and Pepper, Pr.	15.50
Creamer, Flat or Footed	3.50	Sandwich Server, Center Handle	12.50
Cup	2.00	Saucer	1.00
Ice or Butter Tub	12.00	Sherbet	2.50
Pitcher, 7 5/8", 58 oz.	12.50	Sugar, Flat or Footed	3.50
Plate, 6" Sherbet	1.00	Tumbler, 3", 5 oz. Juice	2.50
		Tumbler, 5", 9 oz. Water	3.50

Please refer to Foreword for pricing information

STARLIGHT   HAZEL ATLAS GLASS COMPANY 1938-1940

Colors: Crystal, pink; some white, cobalt.

Some people buy the bowls from this pattern to supplement other patterns. One lady sang the praises of the large bowl as a must for the tossed salad at their family reunions. As I've seen smaller punch bowls, I assume it could be used in that capacity!

These three pieces are all the white I've seen; and I've only seen bowls in the cobalt color.

Please notice the crystal sherbet exists! It was pictured last time but omitted from the listing!

	Crystal/ White	Pink	Cobalt		Crystal/ White	Pink	Cobalt
Bowl, 5½" Cereal	2.00	3.00		Plate, 9" Dinner	3.50	5.00	
*Bowl, 8½", Closed Handles	3.00	6.50	5.00	Plate, 13" Sandwich	3.50	5.25	
				Relish Dish	2.50	4.50	
Bowl, 11½" Salad	10.00	12.50	15.00	Salt and Pepper, Pr.	12.50		
Plate, 6" Bread and Butter	2.00	2.25		Saucer	1.00	2.00	
Creamer, Oval	3.00	*		Sherbet,	3.50		
Cup	2.50	2.50		Sugar, Oval	3.00		
Plate, 8½" Luncheon	2.00	2.75					

STRAWBERRY   U.S. GLASS COMPANY Early 1930's

Colors: Pink, green, crystal; some iridized.

Collector's have placed a couple of designs under the Strawberry label. There are pieces which have cherries in place of the strawberries. Dealers now refer to these pieces as CHERRYBERRY rather than having to explain that it's the Strawberry pattern with the cherry design. I have listed three items of Cherryberry separately due to the large price differential of these from those of Strawberry.

The oversized sugar bowl does not have handles. I have letters from people who found it sans top and have believed it to be a spooner. You may use it as such; but it has a cover and was intended to be a large sugar.

A new bowl has been found which is 6¼" wide and 2" deep.

Crystal and iridized pitchers are located on the rare page in the back.

New collectors should know that butter bases are plain glass except for a rayed motif in the bottom; only the top has any pattern.

	Pink, Green, Crystal			Pink, Green, Crystal
Bowl, 4" Berry	4.50	Pickle Dish, 8¼" Oval		7.00
Bowl, 6¼", 2" Deep	20.00	***Pitcher, 7¾" (Iridescent $125.00)		92.50
Bowl, 6½" Deep Salad	7.50	Plate, 6" Sherbet		3.50
*Bowl, 7½" Deep Berry	9.50	Plate, 7½" Salad		6.50
**Butter Dish and Cover	97.50	Sherbet		5.50
Comport, 5¾"	8.00	Sugar, Small, Open		10.00
Creamer, Small	8.00	Sugar Large		9.00
Creamer, Large, 4 5/8"	10.00	Sugar Cover		12.50
Olive Dish, 5", One Handled	6.50	****Tumbler, 3 5/8", 9 oz.		13.50

   *Iridescent — 7.50
  **Cherry Motif — 137.50
 ***Cherry Motif — 127.50
****Cherry Motif — 16.00

Please refer to Foreword for pricing information

177

SUNFLOWER JEANNETTE GLASS COMPANY

Colors: Pink, green, some delphite.

Popularity of Sunflower has increased tremendously, especially in green. Even the ever abundant cake plate has gone up in price. I once found about twenty-five of these at a garage sale for 50 cents and only bought ten. It took me the better part of two years to get $2.00 for them! I've finally found out why this particular cake plate is so plentiful. A former grocer from the Depression era remembers these being packed in twenty pound bags of flour over a period of three or four years. There surely was a whole lot of baking going on then!

The rare 7″ Sunflower trivet is pictured on the 2nd edition cover photo in the back.

A few pieces of delphite Sunflower are showing up such as sugars, creamers and ash trays. Those odd mustard and old mayonnaise colored pieces of Sunflower are still unique to my knowledge.

	Pink/Green		Pink/Green
*Ash Tray, 5″ Center Design Only	4.50	Saucer	2.00
Cake Plate, 10″, 3 Legs	5.00	Sugar (Opaque $75.00)	5.50
Creamer (Opaque 75.00)	5.50	Tumbler, 4¾″, 8 oz. Footed	10.50
Cup	5.00	Trivet, 7″, 3 Legs, Turned Up Edge	77.50
Plate, 9″ Dinner	5.50		

*Found in Ultra-Marine $16.50
**Delphite 35.00

179

SWANKY SWIGS 1930's-1950's

Swanky Swigs are another of the oddities of the era that Depression Glass collectors are now seeking. Originally, these little glasses came with Kraft cheese products contained therein. Notice the "Pimento" label still attached to the yellow 'Forget-Me-Not' design; on the 4th row is an "Olive Pimento" label on a red 'Kiddie Cup' design. Pattern identification of these little glasses I attribute to Ian Warner who has written numerous articles on them for the various trade papers.

I grew up with these. Two whole shelves of our cupboard were lined with them since my mother ran a nursery/daycare center for 35 children under five. These were the "glasses" used daily for the wee ones meal times; so, only a couple of dozen or so remained in the attic; and when I decided to include them in the book, we really had to do some searching around to find the various ones. In three years of searching, this is what we've found. At present, I'm pricing only those pictured. You may well find others not pictured. I'm also presenting a range of price rather than one set price. As I travel the country now, it seems the price gotten in one place might be the straw to break the camel's back in the next!

The large red sailboat and the blue are definitely Swanky Swigs; the two between are questionable still.

Thanks to Mrs. Robert Marshall, Jr., for sharing part of her collection with us.

Top Picture

Top Row	Band No. 1	Red & Black	3 3/8"	1.50 - 2.50
	Band No. 2	" "	4¾"	2.50 - 3.50
		" "	3 3/8"	2.00 - 3.00
	Band No. 3	Blue & White	3 3/8"	2.00 - 3.00
	Circle & Dot:	Blue, Red	4¾"	5.00 - 6.00
		Red	3½"	2.00 - 3.00
		Black, Blue	3½"	4.00 - 5.00
		Green	3½"	2.00 - 3.00
2nd Row	Star:	Red	4¾"	3.00 - 4.00
		Red, Blue, Green, Black	3½"	2.00 - 3.00
	Checkerboard	Blue, Red	3½"	7.50 - 9.00
	Sailboat	Red	4½"	4.00 - 5.00
		Red, Blue	3½"	5.00 - 6.00
		Blue	3½"	3.00 - 4.00
3rd Row	Tulip No. 1	Green	4½"	4.00 - 5.00
		Green	3½"	2.00 - 3.00
		Red	4½"	4.00 - 5.00
		Red, Dark Blue	3½"	2.00 - 3.00
		Black	3½"	2.50 - 3.50
		Blue (Light)	4½"	4.00 - 5.00
	Tulip No. 2	Black	3½"	8.00 - 9.00
	Carnival	Blue, Red	3½"	2.00 - 3.00
4th Row	Carnival	Green, Yellow	3½"	7.00 - 8.00
	Tulip No. 3	Red, Dk. Bl., Yel., Lt. Bl.	3½"	1.00 - 2.00
	Posey: Tulip, Violet	Red, Blue	3½"	1.00 - 2.00
	Jonquil	Yellow	3½"	1.50 - 2.50

Second Picture

Top Row	Posey: Cornflower No. 1	Blue	3½"	1.00 - 2.00
	Cornflower No. 2	Dk. Blue, Lt. Blue, Red, Yellow	3½"	1.00 - 2.00
	Forget-Me-Not	Lt. Blue; Dk. Blue;	3½"	1.00 - 2.00
		Red, Yellow,	3½"	1.00 - 2.00
2nd Row	Daisy	Red & White; Red, White & Green	3¾"	.75 - 1.50
	Bustlin' Betsy	Green, Blue	3¾"	1.00 - 2.00
		Blue	3¼"	3.00 - 4.00
		Orange	3¾"	1.50 - 2.50
		Yellow, Red, Brown	3¾"	1.00 - 2.00
3rd Row	Antique Pattern:			
	Clock & Coal Scuttle	Brown	3¾"	1.00 - 2.00
	Lamp & Kettle	Blue	3¾"	1.00 - 2.00
	Coffee Grinder & Plate	Green	3¾"	1.00 - 2.00
	Spinning Wheel & Bellows	Red	3¾"	1.00 - 2.00
	Coffee Pot & Trivet	Black	3¾"	1.00 - 2.00
	Churn & Cradle	Orange	3¾"	1.00 - 2.00
4th Row	Kiddie Cup:			
	Dog & Rooster	Orange	3¾"	1.00 - 2.00
	Cat & Rabbit	Green	3¾"	.75 - 1.75
	Bear & Pig	Blue	3¾"	.75 - 1.75
	Bird & Elephant	Red	3¾"	.75 - 1.75
	Squirrel & Deer	Brown	3¾"	.75 - 1.75
	Duck & Horse	Black	3¾"	.75 - 1.75

SWIRL, "PETAL SWIRL"   JEANNETTE GLASS COMPANY 1937-1938

Colors: Pink, ultra-marine, delphite, some amber, ice-blue.

If you collect the ultra-marine color in Swirl you'll be aware that color variations do occur in many pieces; some are more blue than green and vise versa.

Collectors of pink swirl aren't as numerous as those of ultra-marine; but they're having a tough time finding the candy dishes, butter dishes and lug soups in their color. Shakers in pink haven't yet turned up.

There is a 48 oz. footed pitcher in ultra-marine to look for as well as the problemsome flat iced teas!

Neophites please notice there are round and fluted edged swirl plates and that coasters are plain of edge but have the typical concentric rings as a bottom motif. (They also came with small General Tires around them as advertising pieces for said company.)

	Pink	Ultra-Marine	Delphite
Ash Tray, 5 3/8″	5.00		
Bowl, 5¼″ Cereal	4.00	6.00	7.00
Bowl, 9″ Salad	7.50	12.50	15.00
Bowl, 10″ Footed, Closed Handles		17.50	
Bowl, 10½″ Console, Footed	10.00	15.00	
Butter Dish	125.00	185.00	
Candleholders, Double Branch, Pr.	20.00	17.50	
Candleholders, Single Branch, Pr.			75.00
Candy Dish, Open, 3 Legs	2.25	4.75	
Candy Dish with Cover	45.00	57.50	
Coaster, 1″ x 3¼″	4.50	5.50	
Creamer, Footed	4.50	6.50	7.50
Cup	3.00	4.50	5.00
Pitcher, 48 oz. footed		500.00	
Plate, 6½″ Sherbet	1.50	2.25	3.00
Plate, 7¼″	3.25	5.00	
Plate, 8″ Salad	3.50	6.00	4.50
Plate, 9¼″ Dinner	4.50	6.50	5.50
Plate, 10½″			10.00
Plate, 12½″ Sandwich	5.50	9.50	
Platter, 12″ Oval			19.50
Salt and Pepper, Pr.		20.00	
Saucer	1.50	1.75	2.25
Sherbet, Low Footed	2.50	4.50	
Soup — Tab Handles, (Lug)	9.00	9.50	
Sugar, Footed	4.50	6.50	7.50
Tumbler, 4″, 9 oz.	6.50	9.50	
Tumbler, 4 5/8″, 9 oz.	8.00		
Tumbler, 4¾″, 12 oz.	12.50	22.50	
Tumbler, 9 oz., Footed	9.50	12.50	
Vase, 6½″, Footed	5.50	12.50	
Vase, 8½″, Footed		14.50	

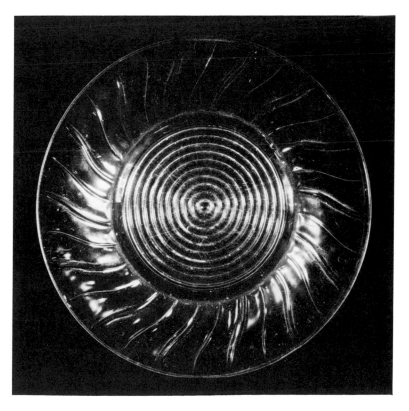

183

TEA ROOM INDIANA GLASS COMPANY 1926-1931

Colors: Pink, green, amber, some crystal.

Tea Room was designed to be used in the "tea rooms" and "ice cream parlors" of the day. Hence its name, its heavy durability and its abundance of soda fountain items. Plates, cups and saucers are relatively scarce items when compared to the other pieces available in the pattern.

To date there are only four things found in amber: pitcher, tumbler, creamer and sugar. The unusual amber and crystal pitchers are photographed on the cover.

The little object in the foreground in pink is the mustard jar sans lid. The lid is notched to accommodate a spreader.

After examining 96 pieces in their sealed-from-the-factory state and finding only 8 in mint condition, I feel safe in saying these jutting edges came out of the molds rough; however, prices here are still for MINT condition glass; a chip or flake means damage and lower price!

Lamps appear harder to find than first thought.

Notice the two styles of sugars and creamers. The flat-sided one is more difficult in my area.

	Pink/Green		Pink/Green
Bowl, 7½" Banana Split	8.50	*Plate, 8¼" Luncheon	16.50
Bowl, 8½" Celery	8.50	Plate, 10½", Two Handled	17.50
Bowl, 8¾" Deep Salad	25.00	Relish, Divided	7.50
Bowl, 9½" Oval Vegetable	32.50	Salt and Pepper, Pr.	27.50
Candlestick, Low, Pr.	19.50	*Saucer	8.50
Creamer, 4" (Amber $35.00)	7.50	Sherbet, Three Styles	7.50
Creamer, Rectangular	9.00	Sugar, 4" (Amber $35.00)	8.50
Creamer and Sugar on Tray, 3½"	27.50	Sugar, Rectangular	9.00
*Cup	12.50	Sugar, Flat with Cover	17.50
Goblet, 9 oz.	15.00	Sundae, Footed	9.50
Ice Bucket	22.50	Tumbler, 8½ oz.	15.00
Lamp, 9" Electric	27.50	Tumbler, 6 oz., Footed	10.50
Mustard, Covered	42.50	Tumbler, 9 oz., Footed (Amber $40.00)	10.50
Parfait	7.50	Tumbler, 11 oz., Footed	12.50
Pitcher, 64 oz. (Amber $177.50)	67.50	Tumbler, 12 oz., Footed	17.50
Plate, 6½" Sherbet	6.50	Vase, 9" Ruffled Edge or Straight	17.50
		Vase, 11", Ruffled Edge or Straight	21.50

*Prices for absolute mint pieces.

185

THISTLE MACBETH-EVANS 1929-1930

Colors: Pink, green, some yellow, crystal.

A prickly problem in this pattern is posed by its paucity of pieces! Don't mind me, I get a little giddy about this stage of writing every book. It just seemed that this pattern presents the perfect place for "pointedly" using alliteration.

Though Thistle is a minor pattern with few pieces, I am surprised by its number of devotees!

The large Thistle bowl, which should read 10¼" across, is harder to find in pink than the practically impossible green.

That yellow cereal bowl remains the only piece to surface in yellow.

New collectors will notice this resembles Dogwood because the same molds were used for both. However, Dogwood sports a pitcher and tumblers. We're still hoping for Thistle.

The heavy pink butter dish being frequently found is a new copy of an old Pattern Glass Butter Dish and not part of this pattern.

	Pink	Green		Pink	Green
Bowl, 5½" Cereal	7.50	8.50	Plate, 8" Luncheon	5.50	6.50
Bowl, 10¼" Large Fruit	67.50	57.50	Plate, 10¼" Grill	8.50	9.50
Cup, Thin	7.50	8.00	Plate, 13" Heavy Cake	47.50	57.50
			Saucer	3.00	4.00

"THUMBPRINT", PEAR OPTIC FEDERAL GLASS COMPANY 1929-1930

Color: Green.

So many people have had difficulty in finding this pattern in my book, I've moved it to its common name location.

There has not been enough "Thumprint" found to make it interesting to collectors. Of course, if a pitcher were to be found for all those sizes of tumblers, that could change somewhat!

People searching for luncheon sets in Pear Optic report difficulty in finding creamers, sugars and shakers. I traveled to a back corner of Florida to find the sherbet for the picture.

See the explanation under Raindrops in order to distinguish between these two patterns.

	Green		Green
Bowl, 4¾" Berry	1.50	Salt and Pepper, Pr.	12.50
Bowl, 5" Cereal	1.75	Saucer	1.00
Bowl, 8" Large Berry	4.00	Sherbet	3.50
Creamer, Footed	3.00	Sugar, Footed	3.00
Cup	2.50	Tumbler, 4", 5 oz.	2.50
Plate, 6" Sherbet	1.00	Tumbler, 5", 10 oz.	2.75
Plate, 8" Luncheon	2.00	Tumbler, 5½", 12 oz.	3.50
Plate, 9¼" Dinner	3.00	Whiskey, 2¼", 1 oz.	3.00

TWISTED OPTIC IMPERIAL GLASS COMPANY 1927-1930

Colors: Pink, green, amber.

The center handled server pictured belongs to Spiral. Twisted Optic's center handled server has an opened space in the handle for gripping (Y shaped) and the spirals appear to go left, the wrong direction for this pattern. (See Spiral explanation).

I have seen sherbet plates and sherbets in canary yellow and medium blue.

	Pink, Amber, Green		Pink, Amber, Green
Bowl, 4¾" Cream Soup	4.50	Plate, 8" Luncheon	2.00
Bowl, 5" Cereal	1.50	Preserve (Same as Candy but with	
Bowl, 7" Salad or Soup	3.50	Slot in lid)	15.00
Candlesticks, 3", Pr.	8.50	Sandwich Server, Center Handle	9.50
Candy Jar and Cover	12.50	Sandwich Server, Two Handled	4.50
Creamer	4.50	Saucer	1.00
Cup	2.00	Sherbet	2.50
Pitcher, 64 oz.	14.50	Sugar	4.50
Plate, 6" Sherbet	1.25	Tumbler, 4½", 9 oz.	3.00
Plate, 7" Salad	1.50	Tumbler, 5¼", 12 oz.	4.00

VITROCK, "FLOWER RIM" HOCKING GLASS COMPANY 1934-1937

Colors: White and fired-on colors.

Collectors most often refer to the flower bedecked items as Vitrock. Hocking referred to their white line of glassware, flower strewn or not, as Vitrock just as Platonite was a line of glassware at Hazel Atlas. Therefore, when meaning this particular pattern, calling it "Flower Rim" is actually the better idea. Time will tell whether collectors will do so or not.

The only really difficult piece that collectors question me about seeing is the cream soup. Other items may be in short supply, but it will take time and a few more collectors for these to be ascertained.

	White		White
Bowl, Berry, 4"	1.50	Plate, Luncheon, 8¾"	1.75
Bowl, Cream Soup, 5½"	3.00	Plate, Soup, 9"	2.00
Bowl, Fruit, 6"	2.50	Plate, Dinner, 10"	2.50
Bowl, Cereal, 7½"	1.50	Platter, 11½"	4.00
Bowl, Vegetable, 9½"	4.00	Saucer	.75
Creamer, Oval	2.50	Sugar, Oval	2.50
Cup	1.50		
Plate, Salad, 7¼"	1.00		

189

"VICTORY" DIAMOND GLASS-WARE COMPANY 1929-1932

Colors: Amber, green, pink; some cobalt blue; black.

"Victory" is better quality glassware than that generally thought of as being Depression Glass. This is born out by the ground bottoms on the pieces rather than molded ones.

New finds in "Victory" include a 9" oval vegetable, sherbet and 12" platter.

An unusual cobalt blue sandwich server was used for the pattern shot. An occasional piece of black has been found.

The most desirable piece to own seems to be the gravy boat and platter.

Few console sets still have the painted decorations as they wore off easily with use. It's no great loss to my thinking; but some Art Deco enthusiasts admire that touch.

However, gold trimmed pink and green goblets are outstanding. Watch for those.

	Pink, Green	Amber, Blue
Bowl, 6½", Cereal	5.00	6.00
Bowl, 8½" Flat Soup	6.00	7.00
Bowl, 9", Oval Vegetable	12.50	17.50
Bowl, 12", Console	12.50	17.50
Candlesticks, 3", Pr.	12.50	17.50
Cheese & Cracker Set, 12" Indented Plate & Compote	15.00	
Comport, 6" Tall, 6¾" Diameter	6.00	8.00
Creamer	4.50	7.50
Cup	3.00	3.50
Goblet, 5", 7 oz.	10.00	15.00
Gravy Boat and Platter	67.50	77.50
Mayonnaise Set: 3½" Tall, 5½" Across, 8½" Indented Plate w/Ladle	17.50	27.50
Plate, 6" Bread and Butter	1.50	2.00
Plate, 7" Salad	2.50	3.50
Plate, 8" Luncheon	2.00	3.00
Plate, 9" Dinner	4.00	6.50
Platter, 12"	12.50	17.50
Sandwich Server, Center Handle	12.50	27.50
Saucer	1.25	2.00
Sherbet, Footed	6.00	7.50
Sugar	4.50	7.50

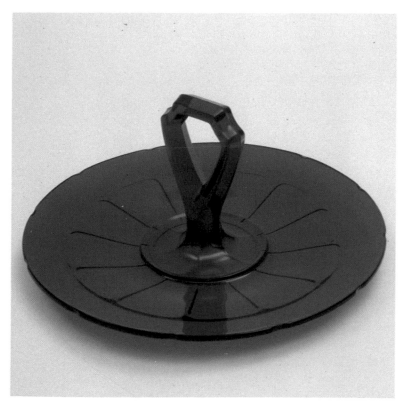

191

WATERFORD, "WAFFLE" HOCKING GLASS COMPANY 1938-1944

Colors: Crystal, pink; some yellow, white; 1950's green.

Crystal Waterford is picking up more fans; so far, the glass is readily available but I wonder how much longer it will be before the pinch is felt in locating cereal bowls?

Pink Waterford has some collectors pulling their hair trying to find butter dishes, pitchers and cereal bowls. The cereal bowl is winning the price race from a percentage standpoint. A juice pitcher in pink has not yet appeared though there are some being found with a "similar" design to Waterford.

To the listing of Waterford having the Miss America shape which has already been discovered (crystal creamer and sugar, pink water goblet complete with three rings encircling the top) you may now add a 3½", 5 oz. juice tumbler in pink.

Reported last time was a sherbet in Waterford that had scallops both top and bottom. Don't forget to look for that.

Notice the yellow salad plate on the left and the ash tray in white which was turned over so you could see the design. The interior of the ash tray is "Dusty Rose" color such as found in Oyster and Pearl fired-on candlesticks. Some later Forest Green pieces can be found.

	Crystal	Pink
Ash Tray, 4"	2.50	4.00
Bowl, 4¾" Berry	2.50	4.50
Bowl, 5½" Cereal	2.50	8.50
Bowl, 8¼" Large Berry	4.00	9.50
Butter Dish and Cover	17.50	167.50
Coaster, 4"	1.50	3.50
Creamer, Oval	2.50	5.50
Creamer, (Miss America Style)	6.00	15.00
Cup	2.50	5.50
Goblets, 5¼", 5 5/8"	5.50	
Goblets, 5½" (Miss America Style)	19.50	35.00
Lamp, 4", Spherical Base	19.50	
Pitcher, 42 oz. Juice, Tilted	12.50	
Pitcher, 80 oz., Ice Lip, Tilted	22.50	97.50
Plate, 6" Sherbet	1.00	2.00
Plate, 7 1/8" Salad	1.25	2.50
Plate, 9 5/8" Dinner	3.50	6.00
Plate, 10¼", Handled Cake	3.00	5.00
Plate, 13¾" Sandwich	3.50	6.50
Salt and Pepper, 2 Types	7.50	
Saucer	1.00	3.00
Sherbet, Footed	2.50	5.00
Sugar	2.50	5.50
Sugar Cover, Oval	2.50	6.00
Sugar (Miss America Style)	6.00	15.00
Tumbler, 3½", 5 oz. Juice		20.00
Tumbler, 4 7/8", 10 oz. Footed	4.00	8.50
Vase, 6¾"	8.00	

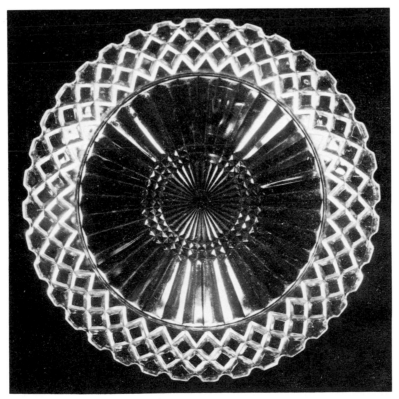

193

WINDSOR, "WINDSOR DIAMOND" JEANNETTE GLASS COMPANY 1936-1946

Colors: Pink, green, crystal; some delphite, amberina red.

If you will refer to the 3rd edition rare items photograph located in the back of this book, you will see the Windsor punch bowl that is made from the large bowl resting atop an inverted comport. Clever idea! It was manufactured to do this, understand; they fit into one another. It probably explains why we find so many more cups than we do saucers. It was packaged with twelve cups. This punch bowl combination is selling presently for a reasonable $20 - $25!

Amberina red continues to show up since a cup, saucer and plate have now been seen.

Prices for pink Windsor have made the largest advance; a limited supply of green seems to have stifled the growth of that color.

This pattern was christened during a time when a certain young king from the house of Windsor captured the sympathies of the world when he gave up his throne in order to marry an American lady he loved. Hail, Edward! Duke of Windsor!

	Crystal	Pink	Green
*Ash Tray, 5¾"	6.50	25.00	37.50
Bowl, 4¾" Berry	1.50	2.50	3.50
Bowl, 5" Cream Soup	3.50	6.50	7.50
Bowl, 5 1/8", 5 3/8" Cereals	2.00	8.00	9.00
Bowl, 7 1/8", Three Legs	3.50	9.50	
Bowl, 8½", Large Berry	3.50	5.50	7.50
Bowl, 9½" Oval Vegetable	4.50	6.50	8.00
Bowl, 10½" Salad	4.00		
Bowl, 12½" Fruit Console	8.00	12.50	17.50
Bowl, 7" x 11¾", Boat Shape	6.50	15.00	17.50
Butter Dish	20.00	27.50	67.50
Cake Plate, 10¾" Ftd.	5.00	7.50	10.00
Cake Plate, 13½" Thick	5.00	6.50	7.50
Candlesticks, 3", Pr.	8.00	12.50	
Candy Jar and Cover	7.50	10.50	
Coaster, 3¼"	2.50	3.50	
Comport	3.00	4.50	
Creamer	3.00	5.50	7.50
Creamer (Shaped as "Holiday")	3.00		
Cup	2.00	3.50	4.50
Pitcher, 4½", 16 oz.	22.50	37.50	
Pitcher, 5", 20 oz.	5.00		
Pitcher, 6¾", 52 oz.	8.00	15.00	32.50
Plate, 6" Sherbet	1.00	1.50	2.00
Plate, 7" Salad	1.50	4.50	5.50
**Plate, 9" Dinner	2.50	5.50	7.50
Plate, 10¼" Sandwich, Handled	3.50	5.50	7.50
Plate, 13 5/8" Chop	4.00	5.50	6.00
Plate, 15½" Serving	5.00		
Platter, 11½" Oval	4.00	6.00	7.00
Relish Platter, 11½", Divided	4.00	6.50	7.50
Salt and Pepper, Pr.	12.50	17.00	27.50
Saucer	1.50	1.50	2.00
Sherbet, Footed	2.00	4.00	5.50
Sugar and Cover	4.00	7.50	10.50
Sugar and Cover (Like "Holiday")	4.00		
Tray, 4" Square	1.50	2.50	4.50
Tray, 4 1/8" x 9"	2.50	4.50	5.50
Tray, 8½" x 9¾"	3.50	5.50	6.00
Tumbler, 3¼", 5 oz.	3.00	6.50	7.00
Tumbler, 4", 9 oz.	4.00	6.75	8.50
Tumbler, 5", 12 oz.	4.00	9.50	15.00
Tumbler, 4" Footed	3.50		
Tumbler, 7¼", Footed	5.00		

*Delphite — 37.50
**Blue — 37.50
**Red — 50.00

Please refer to Foreword for pricing information

Reproductions

NEW "AVOCADO"   INDIANA GLASS COMPANY Tiara Exclusives Line, 1974 . . .

Colors: Pink, frosted pink, yellow, blue, red amethyst, green.

Rumors of a green Avocado pitcher and tumblers finally became reality in the spring of 1979. Thankfully, the green is a darker green than the original color. It is limited in production as a hostess gift item; but the fact that it exists is cause for sharpening your wits. The original green Avocado pitcher is quite rare; so be aware that a new version exists in a darker green color. Sorry it came out too late for the picture!

The pink they made was described under the pattern. It tends to be more orange than the original color. The other colors shown pose little threat as these colors were not made originally.

I understand that Tiara sales counselors tell potential clientelle that their newly made glass is collectible because it is made from old molds. I don't share this view. I feel it's like saying that since you were married in your grandmother's wedding dress, you will have the same happy marriage for the fifty seven years she did. All you can truly say is that you were married in her dress. I think all you can say about the new Avocado is that it was made from the old molds. TIME, SCARCITY and PEOPLE'S WHIM determine collectibility in so far as I'm able to determine it. It's taken nearly fifty years or more for people to turn to collecting Depression Glass---and that's done, in part, because EVERYONE "remembers" it; they had some in their home at one time or another; it has universal appeal. Who is to say what will be collectible in the next hundred years. If we all knew, we could all get rich!

If you like the new Tiara products, then by all means buy them; but don't do so DEPENDING upon their being collectible just because they are made in the image of the old! You have an equal chance, I feel, of going to Las Vegas and DEPENDING upon getting rich at the Black Jack table.

NEW "CHERRY BLOSSOM"   Privately Produced first in 1973 . . .

Colors: Pink, green, blue, delphite.

In 1973 the Depression Glass world was all agog by the appearance of some old looking Cherry child's cups---odd because the cherry design in the bottoms of the cups was hanging upside down, odd because they had oversized handles, odd because so many of them were appearing, odd because a child's butterdish made an appearance about the same time and no such character was originally made. Since then, the little child's butter dishes have appeared in a multitude of colors, some even iridized; and the little cup has been improved only slightly. Even some saucers and plates have appeared; but generally their slipped molding and "off" coloring give them away immediately.

Pictured are the colors made so far in the butter dishes and shakers begun in 1977. Some shakers were dated '77 on the bottom and were marketed at the ridiculous price of $27.95---whopping profit margin! Shortly afterward, the non dated variety appeared. How can you tell new shakers from old--- should you get the one in a million chance to do so?

First, look at the tops. New tops COULD indicate new shakers. Next, notice the protruding ledges beneath the tops. They are squared off juts rather than the nicely rounded scallops on the old (which are pictured under Cherry Blossom pattern). The design on the newer shakers is often weak in spots. Finally, notice how far up inside the shakers the solid glass (next to the foot) remains in the newer shakers have almost half again as much glass in that area? The new shakers appear to be ¼ full of glass before you ever add the salt!

Butter dishes are naturally more deceptive in pink and green since that blue was not an original color. The major flaw in the new butter is that there is ONE band encircling the bottom edge of the butter top; there are TWO bands very close together along the skirt of the old top. Using your tactile sense, the new top has a sharply defined design up inside; the old was glazed and is smooth to touch. The knob on the new is more sharply defined than the smoothly formed knob on the old butter top.

As we go to press a scalloped bottom AOP pitcher and tumbler set are being made. Beware and know your dealer.

197

Reproductions (Con't.)

NEW "MAYFAIR"   Privately Produced 1977 . . .

Colors: Pink, green, blue.

Only the shot glass (which is rare in the original) has been made in this pattern. The green (totally wrong color) and blue are no problem since the shot glasses have never been found in these colors originally. The difficulty comes with the pink.

Generally speaking, the newer shot glass has a heavier over-all look. The bottom area tends to have a thicker rim of glass. Often, the "pink" coloring isn't right; it may be too light, it may be too orange. However, if these cursory examinations fail, there are other points to check.

First, notice the stem of the flower. You have a single stem in the new flower. At the base of the stem in the old glass, the stem separates into an "A" shape. Further, look at the leaves on the stem. In the new design, the leaf itself is hollow with the veins molded in. IN the old glass, the leaf portion is molded in and the veining is left hollow. In the center of the flower, the dots (anther) cluster entirely to one side of the old design and are rather distinct. Nothing like that occurs in the newer version.

NEW "MISS AMERICA"   Privately Produced, 1977 . . .

Colors: Crystal, green, pink, ice blue, red amberina.

The new butter dish in "Miss America" design is probably the best of the newer products; yet there are three distinct differences to be found between the original butter top and the newly made one. Since the value of the butter dish lies in the top, it seems more profitable to examine it.

In the new butter dishes pictured, notice that the panels reaching the edge of the butter bottom tend to have a pronounced curving, skirt-like edge. In the original dish, there is much less curving at the edge of these panels.

Second, pick up the top of the new dish and feel up inside it. If the butter top knob is filled with glass so that it is convex (curved outward), the dish is new; the old inside knob area is concave (curved inward).

Finally, from the underside, look through the top toward the knob. In the original butter dish you would see a perfectly formed multi-sided star; in the newer version, you see distorted rays with no visible points.

Shakers have been made in green, pink and crystal. The shakers will have new tops; but since some old shakers have been given new tops, that isn't conclusive at all. Unscrew the lid. Old shakers have a very neatly formed ridge of glass on which to screw the lid. It overlaps a little and has neatly rounded off ends. Old shakers stand 3 3/8" tall without the lid. New ones stand 3¼" tall. Old shakers have almost a forefinger's depth inside (female finger) or a fraction shy of 2½ inches. New shakers have an inside depth of 2", about the second digit bend of a female's finger. (I'm doing finger depths since most of you will have those with you at the flea market, rather than a tape measure). In men, the old shakers depth covers my knuckle; the new shaker leaves my knuckle exposed. New shakers simply have more glass on the inside of the shaker---something you can spot from twelve feet away! The hobs are more rounded on the newer shaker, particularly near the stem and seams; in the old shaker these areas remained pointedly sharp!

Reproductions (Con't.)

NEW SANDWICH (Indiana)   INDIANA GLASS COMPANY Tiara Exclusive Line 1969 . . .

Colors: Amber, blue, red, crystal.

The smokey blue and amber shown here are representative of Tiara's line of Sandwich which is presently available. (See Sandwich pattern for older amber color).

The bad news is that the crystal has been made now and there are only minute differences in this new and the old. I will list the pieces made in crystal and you can make yourself aware of these re-issues if you collect the crystal Sandwich.

Ash Tray Set
Basket, Handles, 10½"
Bowl, 4" Berry
Bowl, 8"
Butter Dish & Cover
Candlesticks, 8½"
Cup, 9 oz.
Cup (fits indent in oval sandwich plate, 6 oz.)
Decanter & Stopper (10")
Goblet, 8 oz., 5¼"
Pitcher, 68 oz. Fluted Rim, 8" Tall
Plate, 10" Dinner
Plate, 8" Salad
Plate, 8½" x 6¾" Oval Sandwich
Sandwich Tray, Handled
Saucer, 6"
Sherbets
Tray, 10" (Underliner for Wine
    Decanter & Goblets)
Tumbler, 6½" High, 12 oz.

I discussed the red color made in 1969 under the Sandwich heading, Page 170.

See last two paragraphs of text under New Avocado.

NEW "SHARON"   Privately Produced 1976 . . .

Colors: Blue, dark green, light green, pink, burnt umber.

A blue Sharon butter turned up in 1976 and turned my phone line to a liquid fire! Would you believe I still get a few letters and calls about it, now, three years later? The color is Mayfair blue---a fluke and dead giveaway as far as real Sharon is concerned.

When found in similar colors to the old, pink and green, you can immediately tell that the new version has more glass in the top where it changes from pattern to clear glass, a thick, defined ring of glass as opposed to a thin, barely defined ring of glass in the old. The knob of the new dish tends to stick up more. In the old butter dish there's barely room to fit your finger to grasp the knob. The new butter dish has a sharply defined ridge of glass in the bottom around which the top sits. The old butter has such a slight rim that the top easily scoots off the bottom.

In 1977 a "cheese dish" appeared having the same top as the butter and having all the flaws inherent in that top which were discussed in detail above. However, the bottom of this dish was all wrong. It's about half way between a flate plate and a butter dish bottom, bowl shaped; and it is over thick, giving it an awkward appearance. The real cheese bottom was a salad plate with a rim for holding the top. These "round bottom cheese dishes" are but a parody of the old and are easily spotted. We removed the top from one in the picture so you could see its heaviness and its bowl shape.

201

First Edition Cover

Amethyst	Right Center: Royal Lace Sherbet
Blue	Center Front: Princess Cup
	Right Rear: Mayfair Pitcher
Green	Center Middle: Cherry Shakers
	Left Rear: Mayfair Pitcher
Pink	Left Front: Cameo Wine
	Right Front: Cameo Water Tumbler
	Right Front: Cameo Creamer
	Center Middle: Mayfair Footed Bowl
Yellow	Center Rear: Mayfair Pitcher

Second Edition Cover

Amber	Left Center: Madrid Gravy Boat and Platter Left Rear: Parrot Footed and Flat Iced Teas
Amethyst	Left Foreground: Iris Demi-Tasse Cup and Saucer
Blue	Right Foreground: Iris Demi-Tasse Cup and Saucer Center: Floral Sherbet Right Rear: Princess Cookie Jar and Florentine Pitcher
Custard	Left Center: Sunflower Sugar
Green	Left Front: Sunflower Trivet Left Center: Number 612, 9 and 12 oz. Flat Tumblers Center: Cherry Opaque Bowl Left Rear: Floral Juice Pitcher and Mayfair Cookie Jar Right Rear: Princess Footed Pitcher and Tumbler: Mayfair Liqueur
Iridescent	Right Foreground: Iris Demi-Tasse Cup and Saucer
Mustard	Right Center: Sunflower Creamer
Orange	Right Center: Cherry Opaque Bowl (Reddish with yellow rim)
Pink	Center Foreground: Cameo Ice Tub Left Foreground: Adam-Sierra Butter Dish Center: Cameo Shakers Rear Center: Waterford Lamp by Westmoreland (pattern not included) in book, but shown to differentiate from Miss America and English Hobnail)
Red	Left Foreground: Iris Demi-Tasse Cup and Saucer Center: Miss America Goblet
Yellow	Center: Cherry Vegetable Bowl Right Center: Dogwood Cereal Bowl; Adam 8″ Plate, Cup and Saucer Left Rear: Mayfair Juice Pitcher Right Rear: Mayfair Shakers

Third Edition Cover

Amber	Center: Moondrops Etched Butter
	Right Front: Victory Gravy Boat and Platter
	Left Middle: Cherry Blossom Child's Cup and Saucer; Florentine No. 2 Footed Tumbler
Blue	Left Front: Windsor Delphite Ash Tray
	Left Center: Heritage Berry Bowl
	Left Rear: English Hobnail Handled Bowl
	Right Center: Floral Delphite Tumbler
	Right Rear: Rock Crystal Berry on Silver Pedestal
Green	Left Center: Rock Crystal Shaker
	Left Rear: American Pioneer Lamp
	Right Center Front: Heritage Berry Bowl
	Right Center: American Sweetheart Shaker
	Right Rear: Floral Ice Tub
Iridescent	Center: Louisa Carnival Rose Bowl
Pink	Left Rear: Floral Ice Tub
	Right Middle: American Pioneer Covered Jug
Red	Left Middle: Windsor Tumbler
	Center: Cherry Blossom Bowl
	Center Rear: Rock Crystal Fruit Bowl
Yellow	Right Rear: Pyramid Pitcher

Second Edition Rare Pieces

Blue	Left: Moderntone Sugar with Rare Cover Right: Florentine Tumbler
Crystal	Right: Doric and Pansy Creamer and Sugar
Green	Left Foreground: Parrot Hot Plate and Odd Cameo Top Right Foreground: Madrid Ash Tray Left Center: Floral Vase and "S" Pattern Tumbler Center: Dogwood 9½" Bowl Left Rear: Mayfair 6½" Footed Iced Tea Right Rear: Avocado Pitcher
Pink	Center Foreground: Cameo Drip Tray Right Center: Florentine Lemonade Tumbler Left Rear: Doric Footed Pitcher Center Rear: Diamond Quilted Covered Compote Right Rear: Dogwood Pitcher
Yellow	Left Rear: Florentine Juice Pitcher Right Rear: Number 612 Footed Iced Tea

Third Edition Rare Items

Amber	Center Front: "Apple" (like Avocado) Plate
	Right Rear: Rock Crystal Pitcher
Amethyst	Left Rear: Rock Crystal Berry Bowl
Blue	Left Front: Floral Delphite Platter
	Right Center: Moondrops Butter Dish
	Left Rear: Beaded Block Bouquet Vase
	Left Rear: English Hobnail Lamp
Crystal	Left Front: Rock Crystal Salt Dip
	Center Rear: Windsor Punch Bowl and Stand
Green	Right Center: Ring Shaker
Pink	Left Center: Tea Room Mustard
	Center Front: Cherry Blossom 9 Inch Platter
	Center: American Pioneer Covered Casserole
	Right Front: Adam Round Plate and Round Saucer
	Right Center: Floral 9 Inch Comport
Red	Left: Moondrops Butter Dish
Ultramarine	Center: Doric and Pansy Butter Dish and Shakers
	Right Rear: English Hobnail Sherbet

Fourth Edition Rare Items

Blue	Center Front: Fire King Dinnerware Creamer & Princess Cup and Saucer
Crystal	Left Back: Strawberry Pitcher
	Right Back: Floral and Diamond Pitcher
Green	Left Front: Mayfair Water Goblet, 4¾" Sherbet and Moondrops Butter Dish
	Center Middle: Beaded Block Pitcher
	Right Front: Floral 3 oz. Footed Juice, Flat 9 oz. Tumbler, Lincoln Inn Salt and Pepper Shakers
Iridescent	Left Rear: Strawberry Pitcher
Pink	Center Middle: English Hobnail Pitcher
	Center Right: Mayfair 5¼", 4½ oz. Goblet
Red	Center Rear: Moondrops Pitcher, Radiance Pitcher and Rock Crystal Pitcher
Yellow	Center Front: Mayfair Butter Dish
	Center Right: Princess Juice Pitcher

Fourth Edition Cover Description

Amber   Center Front: Radiance Butter Dish
       Center Middle: English Hobnail Pitcher
       Center Back: Tea Room Pitcher

Blue, Light Center Left: Fire King Dinnerware Juice Pitcher
  Cobalt Center Right: Radiance Handled Decanter

Crystal   Center Back: Tea Room Pitcher

Green   Center Front: Mayfair Butter Dish
       Left Front: Floral Eight Sided Vase
       Left Center: Floral Dresser Set
       Right Center: Mayfair Juice Pitcher
       Left Rear: Rock Crystal 64 oz. Pitcher

Pink   Left Front: Mayfair Footed Shaker, 1 oz. Liqueur & Round Cup and
       Saucer
       Left Rear: Colonial Bead Top Pitcher
       Right Rear: Princess Footed Pitcher

Red   Center Middle: English Hobnail Pitcher
Yellow   Right Front: Mayfair Sugar and Lid
       Right Front: Cameo Butter Dish and Lid
       Right Rear: Footed Pitcher

Depression Glass Publications

Depression Glass Daze
Nora Koch, Editor
P.O. Box 57 F
Otisville, Michigan 48463
($7.00 year)

Glass Review
Barbara Schaeffer, Editor
P.O. Box 2315 F
Costa Mesa, California 92626
($9.50 year)

Obsession in Depression
Don and Norma Weaver, Editors
20415 Harvest Avenue, Dept. F
Lakewood, California 90715
($6.00 year)